Accounting Database Desi[g]
(Accounting Infor[mation])
Derek Liew

Copyrig[ht]

MW01518625

About the Author

The author is an ACCA qualified Accountant. He has vast technical knowledge in database design and development, with more than 5 years research experience in database design, especially in the area of accounting system design. The author is an experienced user of various accounting application and ERP system.

Comments may be directed to the author at: derek@accountingdes.com
ebook format can be downloaded at : http://www.accountingdes.com

Acknowledgements

To my special friend, Deric Chan, who has brought me out from the nutshell by buying me my first computer book on my 26th birthday. I have found my inspiration in learning the power of SQL. Thank you for introducing me into the world of programming and most of all, for being my best friend.

To my life partner, Sook Kuan, who has taught me to be patient, especially when I'm driving has definitely proves useful in completing my research and finish writing this book.

To my mum, who has provided more help and support than I had expected. Beyond her endless patience and willingness to allow me to pursue my dream, she has given me the greatest gifts: constancy and understanding.

Table of Contents

Chapter 4   Developing the Purchase Table

Chapter 5   Developing the Sales Table

Chapter 6   Developing the Cash Table

Chapter 7   Developing the Asset Table

Chapter 8   Creating Reports from Journals Table

Chapter 9   Creating Reports from Inventory Table

Chapter 10   Creating Reports from Purchase Table

Chapter 11   Creating Reports from Sales Table

Chapter 12   Creating Reports from Cash Table

Chapter 13 Creating Reports from Asset Table

In our modern world today, it is undisputable fact, that most of the corporate world has and is continuously changing and adapting to new technology, especially in the area of computerization, in order to remain competitive in the business world. One of the greatest importances in any corporate industry is adopting a robust and powerful accounting application, that are not just user-friendly, but capable of providing the flexibility and scalability needed in a rapid changing environment.

A powerful accounting application depends fundamentally on a well structured and designed database. The traditional method of designing and creating a flat-file database is no longer viable and economical, as it has numerous flaw and limitation comparing to a relational database. Most of the existing database today, are developed using the relational database management system (RDBMS) approach, of which it is capable of enforcing greater data integrity and consistency, maximizing storage space efficiency and eliminating redundant data.

What Is This Book Is About?

This book will introduce the concept of normalization, adopting the first normal form to third normal form approach in designing and developing an accounting database. We begin to learn how to design and build a group of fundamental tables, representative of each accounting modules that forms the foundation of an accounting database. We learn how to normalize tables, by continuously adding and changing key fields, as we progress from one chapter to the next.

We'll then discuss the function of primary key (PK) and foreign key (FK) in each tables, and the use of building relationship in the Database Diagram. Finally, we'll walk you through creating query to produce report using the SQL Query Analyzer.

Who This Book Is For?

This book is targeted for database developer, database administrator, accountant and university students, who wants to increase their knowledge and skill set in designing and developing a relational accounting database, and have interest in writing SQL query for accounting reports.

This book assumes you are an inexperienced user of Microsoft SQL Server, and will guide you how to install Microsoft SQL Server and how to use SQL Query Analyzer to create query to generate accounting reports.

A basic understanding of relational database concepts will be advantageous, but is not assumed, as it is covered in this book. It is also not assumed that the reader of this book has any experience working with SQL, but will be helpful if you already have the knowledge.

What You Need To Use This Book

You will need a copy of Microsoft SQL Server (at least version 7.0 and above), depending on the type of operating system installed in your workstation. In our exercise, Microsoft SQL Server 2000 for Personal Edition is used. Your workstation can be Windows 98, Window NT 4.0, Windows 2000 and Windows XP if you wish to install Microsoft SQL Server 2000 for Personal Edition.

All code and samples in this book were developed and tested on workstation running Windows XP Professional Edition (SP2).

Conventions

To help you in better understanding this book, different typefaces is used to differentiate between SQL code and regular English, and also help you to identify key concepts.

Text that you will type on your screen should appear in courier new type.

How It Works

After trying out the queries, there will be a further explanation, to help you relate what you have done to what you have just learned.

Chapter 1

Database Design

Database

A database is a place where data are stored in columns, and rows in a table, just like a spreadsheet, a database consist of one or several tables. A table consists of many columns, known as fields, and each field consist of many rows, called records. Data stored in a table, can be retrieved, updated or even deleted through executing a set of instruction to a database. This set of instruction is what we call SQL statement.

When the first database was created, its design was not in perfect form. The model of the design was to store data in a single stream of bytes. This is known as a flat-file database. A flat-file database is inefficient, given the lack of scalability and storage capacity.

Relational Database

A relational database model is designed to contain several tables that can be joined together via the use of common related fields. The link of two or more tables is achieved through the use of primary key and foreign keys, known as a relationship. The advantage of a relational database over a flat-file database is its ability to store data in different tables, with minimal duplication.

Primary Key (PK)

A primary key is an identifier that uniquely identifies a record stored in a table. By assigning a primary key to a particular field in a table, we can uniquely retrieve, update or delete certain records from a table. A primary key, can relate to other primary key created in another table. A primary field cannot be null, means it must be populated with value. A user cannot insert a value in a primary field twice, as a primary field is a unique field, and it cannot contain two rows of records with the same value.

Foreign Key (FK)

A primary key is known as a foreign key, if it links to a primary key of another table. A value entered in a foreign field, should be the same value entered in the primary field of another table. You could not enter a value as a foreign key that are not initially entered or exist in a primary field of another table.

Normalization Concept

Normalization is a process that shows the method or way of designing a well-structured database. Under normalization methodology, we can restructure database by simply following the below main three steps:

1) First Normal Form
2) Second Normal Form
3) Third Normal Form

1) First Normal Form

In the first normal form, a database designer is required to identify the type and group of data that each data item will fall in, and then decide which data should be used as the basis of creating individual table to contain them. Let's take an example of creating a phone book database. A phone book, generally consist of name, date of birth, address, phone number, place of work, and other details. We know that our main item data is Name and Location. So, we create a table called Name_T to store the name, date of birth, and phone number of each individual. We also create a table called Location_T to hold data on address and place of work.

Our next task, under the first normal form, is to eliminate repeating groups of data. We know that, under the Name_T table, it is very likely that two or more person, may share the same name, and as for the address, it is possible that more than one person could be staying in the same place, therefore we could end up typing the same name or address twice in each of the tables. In order to ensure there is no duplication of data in each table, we need to identify a particular field to be a primary key.

A primary key is a unique identifier that identifies particular records in a table, and it ensures that a value entered in its field can never be re-entered twice. This enforces data integrity and consistency. In our Name_T table, we assign the field Name to be a primary field, and set it as primary key, and change the fieldname Name to Name_ID. We then, set the field address as a primary key, changing its fieldname address to Address_ID. We then create another table called, Customer Details_T table to store the Name_ID and Address_ID field. By assigning the Name and Address as a primary key, we can now have more than one record that shares the same name and location.

2) Second Normal Form

No other non-key field is independent of the primary key. We must ensure that all existing fields in a table must depend on the primary key. We know that the Name_T table, contains the date of birth field, and it is possible that more than one person has the same date of birth, thus, we need to create a separate table specifically to hold the date of birth data, and we rename the date of birth to DOB_ID, and set it as a primary key.

3) Third Normal Form

When we reached the second normal form, we almost complete normalizing our database structure. In the third normal form, it's basically ensuring that all non-key fields are now fully dependent on the primary key. We identify one more field that brings us to our third normal form. We could have more than one person working in the same place, thus, it is logical to create the field place of work as a separate table. We rename the existing fieldname place of work to POW_ID, giving reference to a primary key created in a new table called Place_of_Work_T table.

What is SQL?

SQL, an abbreviation for Structured Query Language, is a language used to execute a set of instruction directed to a database. When you go to an auto-teller machine, to withdraw money, you need to press certain button, to instruct the machine what to do, when you go to the Internet, you use your keyboard or mouse to navigate or search for your favorite website, you are telling your machine what to do. All this are possible with the help of SQL.

It is a universal language that receives instruction from a "front-end" object that will then compile and send the instruction back to a "back-end" object. The front-end object is an application tool, such as VB, C++, and the back-end object, is a database system, that helps to store data. The instruction received from a front-end application, generally perform the following task:

1) Select existing data
2) Insert new data
3) Update existing data
4) Delete existing data

SQL is a language governed by the American National Standards Institute (ANSI), a standard committee that consists of database experts from industry and software vendors. Thus, SQL is a universal and open language, meaning that, it is not owned by any industry.

Transact-SQL

DBMS, or database management system, is a software product that holds and store data. A number of famous DBMS worth noting, are, IBM DB2, MySQL, Sybase Adaptive Server, Oracle, Microsoft Access, and Microsoft SQL Server. These various DBMS, would have their own type of SQL version, generally differ in terms of syntax and features, but, they all complied to the American National Standards Institute (ANSI) SQL Standard.

In our exercise contained in this book, we will be using Microsoft SQL Server as our DBMS in employing the use of Transact Structured Query Language (T-SQL), Microsoft's version of SQL.

Installing Microsoft SQL Server 2000 (Personal Edition)

In order to try out some of the query that we are going to build in subsequent chapter, we need to install the Microsoft SQL Server, at least version 7.0 or higher. For the purpose of our case study, Microsoft SQL Server 2000 for Personal Edition would be used. You can choose to install other version in your workstation, but you need to check the minimum requirement before you begin installing other version of Microsoft SQL Server.

1. To install Microsoft SQL Server 2000 (Personal Edition), insert the SQL Server 2000 CD. If Auto run is not enabled, double-click the Autorun.exe program to begin the installation process.

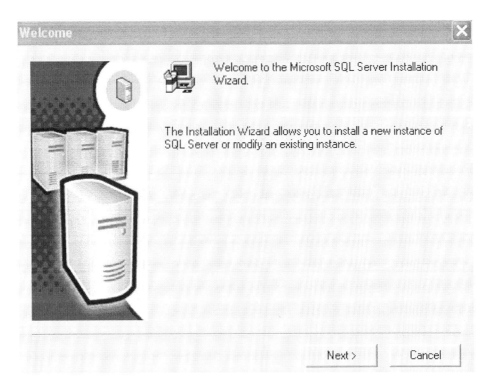

Welcome

Welcome to the Microsoft SQL Server Installation Wizard.

The Installation Wizard allows you to install a new instance of SQL Server or modify an existing instance.

Next >   Cancel

2. Next, you will see a pop-up Welcome screen that will lead you to installing Microsoft SQL Server. Click on the Next button to proceed to the next step.

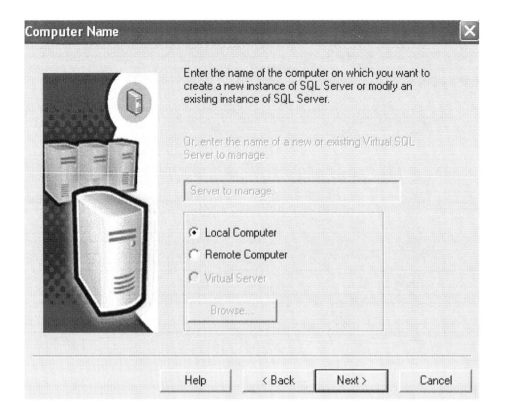

3. The next step allows us to select the name of the computer on which you want to install Microsoft SQL Server. By default, the installation Wizard will select the Local Computer option. As this is where we want to install our Microsoft SQL Server, we will accept the default on this screen. Click on the Next button to proceed to the Installation Selection screen.

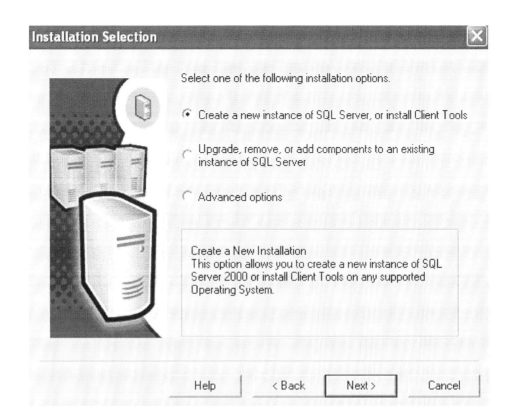

4. Under this screen, we will accept the default option, which will create a new instance of SQL Server in your selected local computer. Click on the Next button to proceed to the next dialog box.

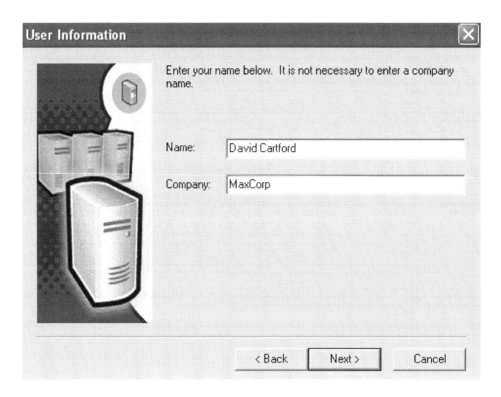

5. In the User Information screen, by default the name and company name will be automatically filled with the same information you have given when you first installed your operating system. If you prefer, you can change the name and company name before you click on the Next button. Click on the Next button once you have changed the name and the company name.

Software License Agreement

 Please read the following License Agreement. Press the PAGE DOWN key to see the rest of the agreement.

ADDENDUM TO THE MICROSOFT END USER LICENSE AGREEMENT FOR MICROSOFT SQL SERVER 2000

The software accompanying this Addendum, Microsoft SQL Server Personal Edition (the "Client Software") is provided to you for use under the terms and conditions of the end user license agreement you acquired with Microsoft SQL Server (Standard or Enterprise Edition) (the "EULA"). Please refer to the EULA for license rights and requirements associated with Client Software. The Client Software is deemed part of the Product (as defined in the EULA), and as such, if you do not have a validly licensed copy of the Product, you are not authorized to use the Client Software. Any capitalized terms used in this Addendum shall have the same meaning as set forth in the EULA, unless otherwise set forth in this Addendum. All terms and conditions of the EULA remain in full force and effect.

Do you accept all the terms of the preceding License Agreement? If you choose No, Setup will close. To install Microsoft SQL Server 2000, you must accept this agreement.

< Back | Yes | No

6. In this screen, you will be required to read the terms and condition of the License Agreement. Press the Page Down key to see the rest of the agreement. Once you have read and agreed to the License Agreement, proceed to the next step by clicking on the Yes button.

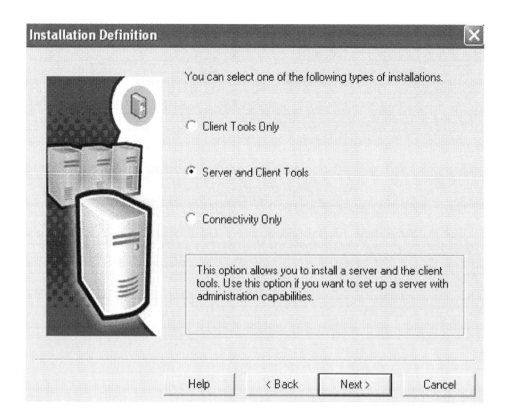

7. Under the Installation Definition screen, you need to select the type of installation that you want to install in your local computer. For our purpose, we will accept the default second option, as we want to make use of the Server and Client tools with administration capabilities. Click the Next button to move to the next screen.

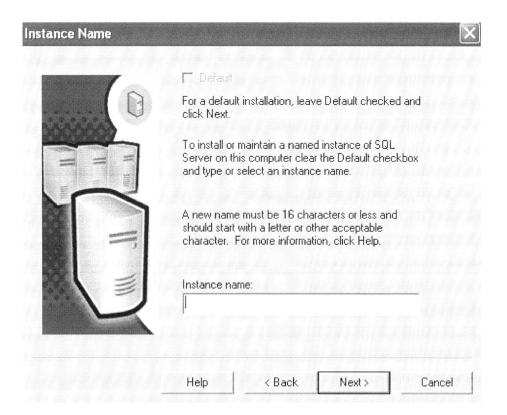

Instance Name

☐ Default

For a default installation, leave Default checked and click Next.

To install or maintain a named instance of SQL Server on this computer clear the Default checkbox and type or select an instance name.

A new name must be 16 characters or less and should start with a letter or other acceptable character. For more information, click Help.

Instance name:

| Help | < Back | Next > | Cancel |

8. The Installation Wizard will detect any installed version of SQL Server on your desktop. If this is your first installation, the default checkbox will be checked by default. If you have previously installed SQL Server, the default checkbox would be grayed out, and you would have to give an instance name for this current installation. The new instance name must be 16 characters or less and should begin with a letter or other acceptable character. Proceed to our next screen once your have given an instance name.

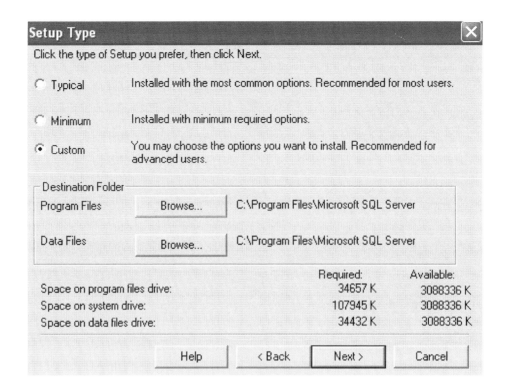

9. On this screen, you are required to select the type of setup. For our purpose, we would want to customize our installation, so let's choose the third option. By default, the program files and data files are directed to windows C drive. If you prefer to relocate the installation folder, you can do so by clicking on the Browse button. Click the Next button once you have completed this step.

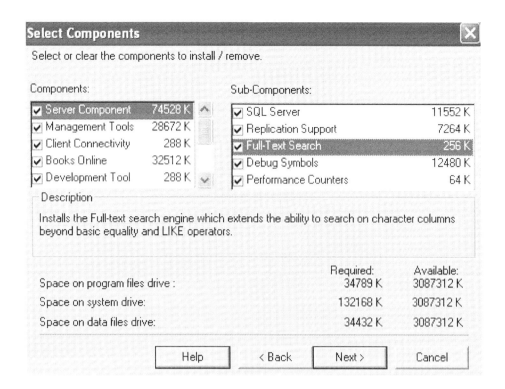

10. Under the Select Component screen, you can view all the main and sub-component that allows you to select and install in your local computer. For our purpose, we will select all components; together will its individual sub-components. Under the Description label, you can view the function of each sub-component by checking on each of the sub-component checkbox. Click next, once you have selected all components.

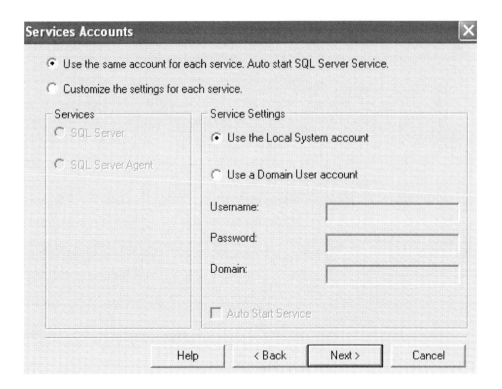

11. Under the Services Accounts screen, you will have the option of selecting different account for each service or assigning the same account for each service. For our purpose, we choose the first option, as this would eliminate any unnecessary problem that a domain user account would normally encounter. Click on the Next button to proceed to our next screen.

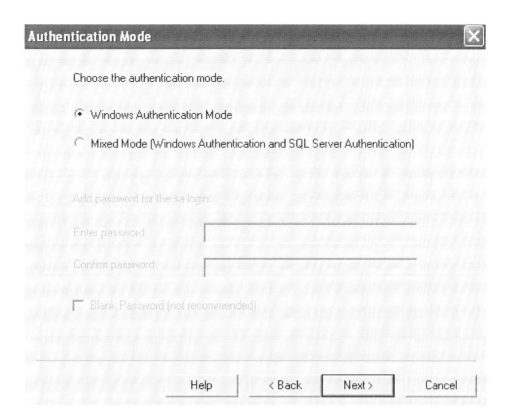

12. This screen allows you to configure the type of authentication mode that you prefer in order to gain access to SQL Server. If you choose the first option, SQL Server will use windows domain user account to verify the authenticity of the user, before granting access to SQL Server. If you choose the second option, SQL Server will require an additional level of validation that would require a user login password. For our purpose, we will select the windows authentication mode option.

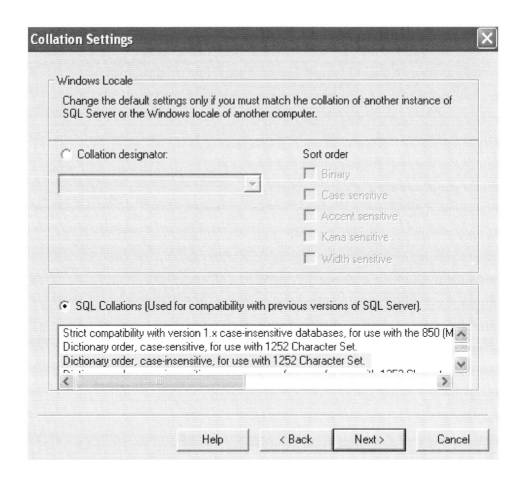

13. Under the Collation Settings, will allow you to specify a set of guidelines that determine how information is being compared and collated in SQL Server. For our purpose, we select the SQL Collations option.

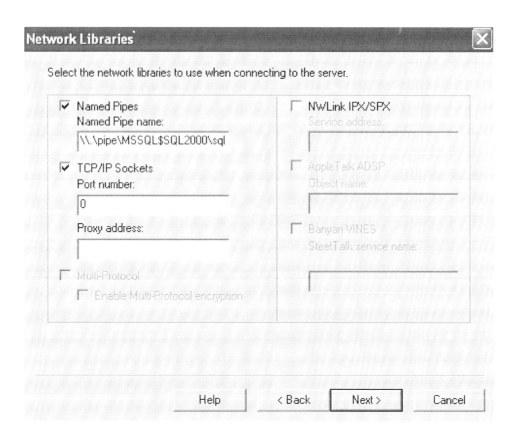

14. SQL Server uses network libraries to pass network packets of information between SQL Server and its clients. By default, SQL Server is configured to listen to packets from clients via the Named Pipes shown on below textbox. If you are installing a named instance, the instance name would appear on the textbox, with a 0 port number specified. If you are installing SQL Server for the first time, the port number 1433 is specified, by default. Once you have specified the Named Pipe name and the port number click on the Next button to move to our next step.

Start Copying Files

Setup has enough information to start copying the program files. If you want to review or change any settings, click Back. If you are satisfied with the settings, click Next to begin copying files.

< Back | Next > | Cancel

15. This is the last setup screen that will begin installing your SQL Server 2000 in your local computer. Click the next button to begin the installation, or click the Back button if you want to change some of the previous setting.

Creating a Database

Before we begin to discuss how to create tables, we need to create a database first.

1. First, open your Enterprise Manager

2. Next, expand the Microsoft SQL Servers root, SQL Server group and then the instance of SQL Server 2000 that you installed.

3. Click on the Database folder, and select Tools from the Menu bar, and then click on Wizard.

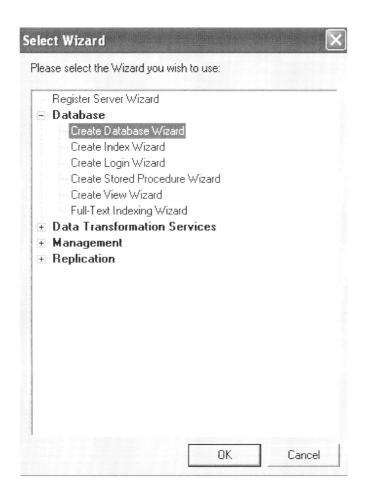

Select Wizard

Please select the Wizard you wish to use:

- Register Server Wizard
- **Database**
  - Create Database Wizard
  - Create Index Wizard
  - Create Login Wizard
  - Create Stored Procedure Wizard
  - Create View Wizard
  - Full-Text Indexing Wizard
- **Data Transformation Services**
- **Management**
- **Replication**

[OK]   [Cancel]

4. Expand the Database, and then select Create Database Wizard. You would see a screen as shown above. Next Click on the OK button to proceed to the next step.

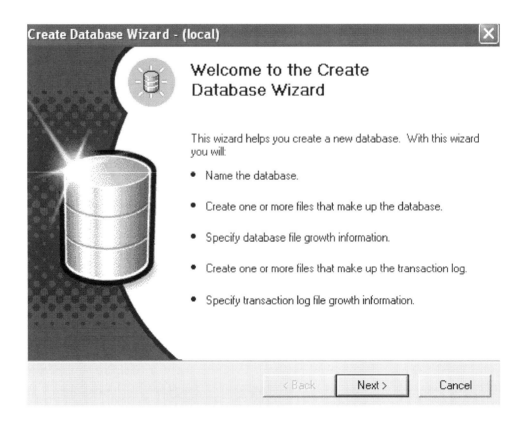

Create Database Wizard - (local)

Welcome to the Create Database Wizard

This wizard helps you create a new database. With this wizard you will:

- Name the database.

- Create one or more files that make up the database.

- Specify database file growth information.

- Create one or more files that make up the transaction log.

- Specify transaction log file growth information.

< Back   Next >   Cancel

5. The next step of the Wizard will show you a summary of the installation guide that we will go through in the following setup process. Click the Next button to proceed to the next screen.

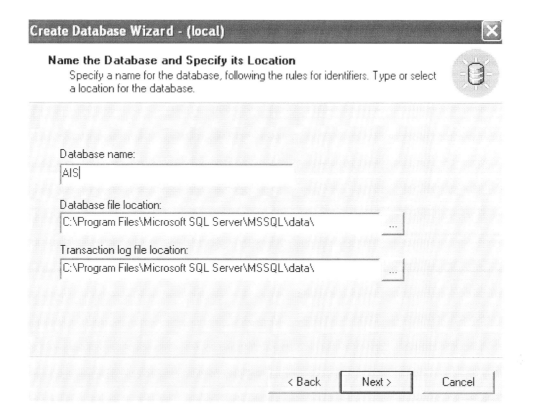

6. In our next screen, we specify a name for our database. Give a name of AIS, which represent the abbreviation of Accounting Information System in the Database name textbox. We can change the default location directory for the database and transaction log file, if you want to, by clicking on the three dotted button beside the textbox. For our purpose, we shall accept the default location for both database and transaction log file. The transaction log file is used to record all transactions performed in your database and can be used for recovery purposes.

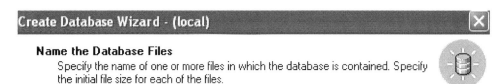

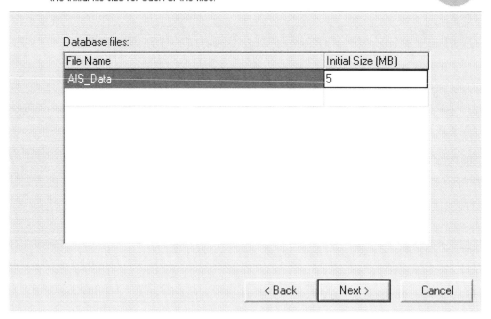

7. Next, we specify the name and the size of our database files. By default, 1 megabyte size is allocated, but we change it to 5 megabytes for our current database. Click on the Next button to proceed to the next screen.

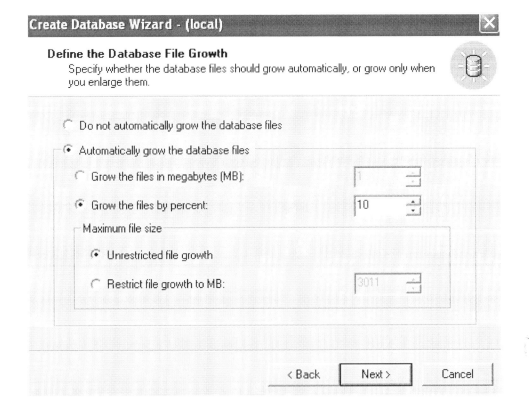

8. We want to allow our database to grow automatically and with unrestricted file size, thus we accept the default options as specified on the above screen. Proceed to the next step by clicking on the Next button.

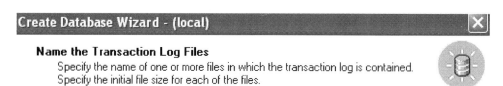

Create Database Wizard - (local)

Name the Transaction Log Files
Specify the name of one or more files in which the transaction log is contained.
Specify the initial file size for each of the files.

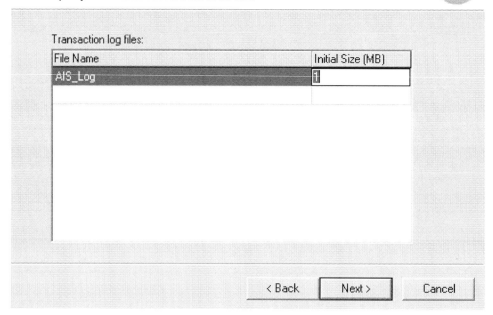

Transaction log files:

File Name	Initial Size (MB)
AIS_Log	1

[< Back] [Next >] [Cancel]

9. We are required to specify the size for our transaction log file. The default 1 megabyte is sufficient for us, thus proceed to the next step by clicking on the Next button.

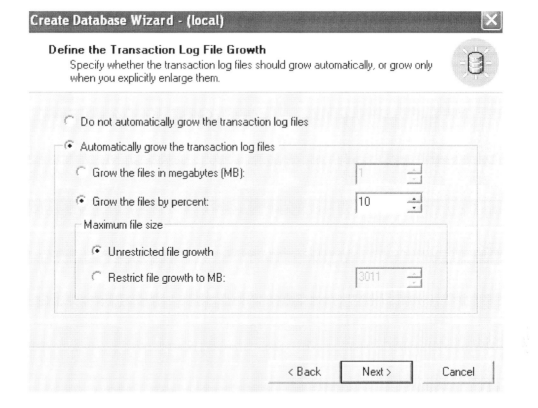

10. Similarly, we also need to specify the size for our transaction log files. By default, the above setting is specified and it should be sufficient for our purpose. Click on the Next button to proceed to the next screen.

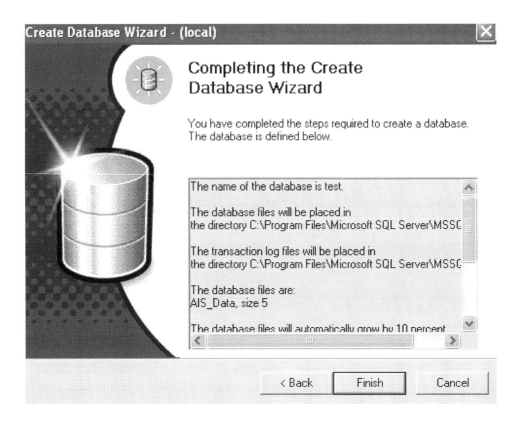

This is the last screen in the Database Wizard. You can now begin to create your first database by clicking on the Finish button, or if you decide to change your previous setting, you can do so by moving backward. Click the Finish button once you are ready to create your database.

Summary

In this Chapter, we have learned what are a database, how to create relationship between tables, and the concept of normalization. We then learned how to install SQL Server and creating a database.

To summaries, in this chapter, we have discussed:

> The advantages of relational database versus a flat-file database

> Normalization Concept (First Normal Form to Third Normal Form)

> How to install SQL Server 2000 (Personal Edition)

> How to create database with Database Wizard

Chapter 2

Developing the Journals Table

Journals Table
Doc_No_VC
Customer_VC
Sales_ID_1
Amount_NU_1
Descrip_VC_I
Sales_ID_2
Amount_NU_2
Descrip_VC_2
Pdt_Name_VC

Normalizing Journal Table

   This chapter will illustrate how an accounting database is being designed. We will begin to adopt the normalization concept to break our table into several tables (First Normal Form to Third Normal Form). Above table contains a list of fields that holds information that consist duplication of data. This table is not normalized and we will begin to identify the key elements that are to become the primary key in a table and as a foreign key in a separate table.

   The Journal table would contain the double-entry information of an entry performed by a user. MaxCorp is in the business of trading computer hardware and software. It needs to have a system to keep track on all its business transaction, and also a system that can produce relevant accounting reports on every close of each month. Dave, the Accountant, would normally raise an invoice to a customer on a Sales Form screen, and information such as date of invoice, product, customer name, pricing would be entered on the face of the Sales Form screen, and would be stored in the above fields created in the Journal Table.

First Normal Form

   We understand that, MaxCorp's customer may receive several invoices in a week from its billing department, and some, merely once in a year, depending on the number of purchases made by its customer. As shown on the table above, currently the Journal Table can only fit in two transactions for each customer and Dave would have to insert a new line of records, having entering the Customer name again, if the same customer buy from MaxCorp for the third time. This is inefficient, as Dave, is repeating groups of data, by entering the customer name twice. To begin our first step of normalization, we will break the Journal Table into a Sales Table and a Journal Table. We will then, assign an Inv_ID_VC fieldname as the primary key in the Sale Table.

By creating a separate Sales Table, Dave would be able to raise as many invoice to a customer without having to repeat its customer name again. By creating a separate Sale Table, we are eliminating duplication of data and making use of the storage space of each field more efficiently, as each customer's name are only created once.

Second Normal Form

We aware that, a customer can buy more than one type of product from MaxCorp, thus, we need to further break up the Journals Table into a Product Table, a Sales Table and a Journals Table. We will assign the fieldname, Pdt_ID_VC as the primary key in the Product Table, and as a foreign key in the Sales Table referencing to a particular product residing in the Product Table. We are establishing a many-to-many relationship between the Sales and Product Table, by connecting these tables via a common field, where a customer may buy different types of products from MaxCorp, and a product could be purchased by different types of customers.

Third Normal Form

So far, we have created two tables out of Journals Table, the Sale Table and Product Table. At this point, our task is incomplete, Dave has voiced his concern on the issue of data integrity. He is worried, especially on numerical fields that hold important figures, vital to the preparation of logical and comprehensive financial reports to MaxCorp's management. He wants to have a database that runs on a real-time basis, where whenever an invoice is issued, an entry would be automatically posted in the Journals, when a collection is made from a customer or payment made to a creditor, an entry would also be posted in the Journals, without having the need for manual entry, simply said, a real-time processing system.

Having understood Dave requisition, we need to redefine the structure of the database design; we know that, he wants a real-time processing for all the posting of journals, the self-creating double-entry records for each level of order processing performed by Dave.

After a brainstorming session with Dave, we understood that, he wants a database that consist a group of tables, representative of each accounting module, to have a direct interface with the Journals Table. The Journal Table is the central repository that records all back-end double-entries performed by the client-application for all order processing transaction, and all front-end transaction performed by the user.

Dave explained, that, for each double-entry performed, a debit, and a credit entry would take place, example, if MaxCorp need to bill a customer, a debit and credit amount would be posted in the Journal Table, debiting an X amount in a Debtor account and crediting the corresponding amount in the Sales account. When he collects from its customer, and then making payment to its creditors on its purchase due, all these transaction would be recorded also as a double-entry in the Journals Table.

With the above knowledge shared by Dave, we need to break the Journals Table further, into another table, known as a Chart of Accounts Table (COA). This Table allows Dave to create account code (GL_ID) that uniquely identify each elements of accounts name, that eventually make up as one of the elements in the COA Table.

Before any transaction is being posted as a double-entry in the Journals Table, user would need to drill-down the dropdown list box, to select the appropriate account code (GL_ID), if it does not exist, user would be prompted to create the account code beforehand in the COA Table. Some of the posting can be pre-defined by the user during set-up stage, for example, double-entry for a customer billing can be pre-defined to debit and credit to a fix Sales and Debtors account, and some transaction would require user selection of account code during order processing process.

A list of important fields with their data type attribute, has been identified in the COA Table, which would have the GL_ID field assigned as primary key, referencing the Journal Table as a foreign key.

Now, Create the COA Table by first Opening the SQL Server 2000, then, select Database | AIS | Table, right click on your mouse, and select New Table as illustrated on below snapshot:

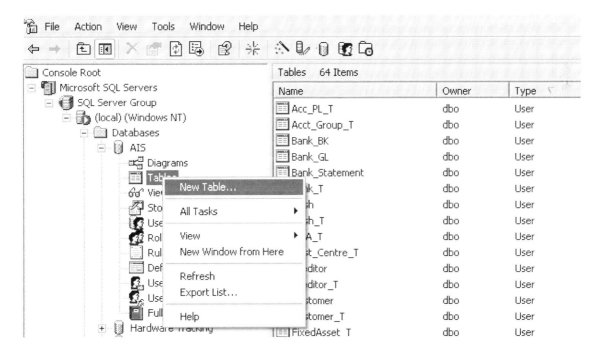

Key in the following fieldnames, data-type, length, and its Allow Null attributes in the COA_T Table as shown below:

COA_T

	Column Name	Data Type	Length	Allow Nulls	
🔑	GL_ID	int	4		
	GL_Name_VC	varchar	20		
	BS_Category_VC	varchar	20		
	Segment_VC	varchar	10	✓	
	Status_BT	bit	1		

Designing Chart of Accounts Table

The GL_Name_VC field would hold the different type of account name, in which are uniquely identified by an account code located in the GL_ID field. The BS_Category_VC field would hold the types of accounts category, to which each individual accounts name will fit in. Segment_VC field stores the different type of business units to be created in MaxCorp. Lastly, user has the option to freeze the account code, by changing its status from active to a non-active account code, preventing the selection of the account code for posting purposes.

Key in the following fieldnames, data-type, length, and its Allow Null attributes in the Journal_T Table as shown below:

Journal_T

	Column Name	Data Type	Length	Allow Nulls
	Doc_No_VC	varchar	10	
	GL_ID	int	4	
	Inv_ID_VC	varchar	10	
	Amount_NU	numeric	9	
	Descrip_VC	varchar	10	
	Date_DT	datetime	8	
	Period_TI	tinyint	1	
	Year_SI	smallint	2	

Designing Journal Table

The Journal table would have a field, called Doc_No_VC that will hold a set of double-entry records performed by a user or by an auto-generated entry performed by the system. Each journal entry would require the following information to be provided, in the remaining fieldnames, the GL_ID field, that will capture the account code of each journal entry, the invoice number (under Inv_ID_VC field) that is assigned as a foreign key, referencing to a particular set of records in the Sale_T table, amount of each transaction posting (under Amount_NU), date of the transaction posting (under Date_DT), Description, Period and Year.

Key in the following fieldnames, data-type, length, and its Allow Null attributes in the Sale_T Table as shown below:

Sale_T *				
Column Name	Data Type	Length	Allow Nulls	
Doc_No_VC	varchar	10		
Pdt_ID_VC	varchar	10		
Cust_Name_VC	varchar	10		
⚷ Inv_ID_VC	varchar	10		

Designing Sales Table

This table contains information on sales transacted with each customer, holding information on product, customer and invoice number. We assign the Inv_ID_VC field as a primary field, as invoice number would be the best candidate for being a unique identifier and as a foreign key in the Journal_T table that will uniquely identify a row of records related to a transaction's double-entry located separately in the Journal Table. The Sales Table merely hold a number of key identifier that are linked to several other tables, namely, the Pdt_ID_VC would link to a Product Table, giving further details, on name, description, category and supplier of each product items. We shall explore further on this table as we develop further in our database design under Chapter 5.

Product_T *				
Column Name	Data Type	Length	Allow Nulls	
⚷ Pdt_ID_VC	varchar	10		
Pdt_Name_VC	varchar	10		

Designing Product Table

We will assign Pdt_ID_VC as the primary key field for Product Table, which holds key information of each product's name. We will get to know the usefulness of account set field, as we touches on Chapter 3 onwards.

Summary

In this Chapter, we have created the Journal Table, and then we learned how to normalize this table into several tables, going through the normalization process, from first normal form to third normal form. In Chapter 3, we will discuss how to normalize the Product Table further, giving us an insight on the types of fields needed in a Product table.

To summaries, in this chapter, we have discussed:

- ➢ The Normalization Concept (First Normal Form to Third Normal Form)

- ➢ The use of Primary and foreign keys

- ➢ The purpose of a Chart of Accounts and its relevant fields

- ➢ The purpose of a Journal Table and its relevant fields

- ➢ The purpose of a Sales Table and its relevant fields

- ➢ The purpose of a Product Table and its relevant fields

Chapter 3

Developing the Inventory Table

Product_T *				
Column Name	Data Type	Length	Allow Nulls	
🔑 Pdt_ID_VC	varchar	20		
Pdt_Name_VC	varchar	30		
Pdt_Descrip_VC	varchar	40	✓	
Pdt_Category_VC	varchar	20		
Cred_ID_VC	varchar	20		
Pdt_AcctSet_VC	varchar	20		

Normalizing Inventory Table

As discussed in Chapter 2, the Product Table was created to keep track on each product item's name, description, supplier code and its account set code. This table is still not in perfect form, as Dave, would also want to keep track on the movement of each of the product sold, the costing method applied on each product items and the pricing of each of its product items. We will again, follow the step-by-step normalization process to further identify key elements that should be broken down further away from the Product Table.

First Normal Form

We know that, not all products in MaxCorp are purchased from the same source of supplier, it could be a product sourced from different supplier or a supplier could also be supplying MaxCorp more than one product type. It is logical, at this point, to create a separate table for supplier, referencing the Product Table via a foreign key named Cred_ID_VC, being a primary key assigned in the Creditor Table.

Second Normal Form

At this stage, we have further identified another key element, the product category, as MaxCorp will also need to group its sale by category, in order to better analyze the marketability and profitability of each product type. We branch out the Pdt_Category_VC field, to create a separate table, named, Product Table_Category, assigning the field Pdt_Category_VC, as the primary key, having linked to the Product Table, as a foreign key.

Third Normal Form

We have not created any field to capture the quantity movement and balance of each product items. Create a table named, Stock_Movement Table to capture the physical movement of each product sold by MaxCorp, and a table named, Stock_Balance Table to monitor the current quantity balance of each product items.

Inventory Table

Stock_Movement_T

Column Name	Data Type	Length	Allow Nulls
Doc_No_VC	varchar	20	
Date_DT	datetime	8	
Pdt_ID_VC	varchar	20	
Qty_NU	numeric	5	
Unit_Price_TI	tinyint	1	
Descrip_VC	varchar	20	

Designing Stock Movement Table

This table would keep track of each product movement in MaxCorp warehouse. A row of records would be inserted into this table when MaxCorp delivers products to its customer, receiving incoming goods from its supplier, or even transferring goods between different warehouse locations. In our table, we only maintain one location for storing MaxCorp's goods, and should MaxCorp expands its business further in future, it may establish branches that would require more than one warehouse to store its product, then MaxCorp may need to create a separate table just to store warehousing information. The Descrip_VC field would accommodate the delivery note and goods receive note numbering for each product items moving in and out from MaxCorp's warehouse.

Enter the following fieldnames, data-type, length, and its Allow Null attributes as shown above:

Stock_Balance_T

	Column Name	Data Type	Length	Allow Nulls	
🔑	Doc_ID_VC	varchar	10		
	Pdt_ID_VC	varchar	20		
	Qty_NU	numeric	5		
	Unit_Price_TI	tinyint	1		
	Date_DT	datetime	8		

Designing Stock Balance Table

This table will hold the latest balance of each product items, after accumulating or deducting the previous balance of each product items, to illustrate this further, assuming that, MaxCorp purchase 2 units of item A at $1.50 each. The system would record this information in this table after updating the Stock_Movement Table. When item A is sold to a customer, the system would then insert a new record in the Stock_Movement Table and will update the balance of item A in Stock_Balance Table simultaneously. For each update in the Stock_Balance Table, the system will first identify the matching product item in the Stock_Balance Table, if it exist, the system would update its quantity and unit price, by replacing its current quantity and unit price, and if, it is a new product item, a new record would then be inserted. This table plays a significant influence on product pricing. We will have a better understanding, as we discuss further on the costing method field created in the Product AccountSet Table.

Enter the following fieldnames, data-type, length, and its Allow Null attributes as shown below:

Product_AccountSet_T

	Column Name	Data Type	Length	Allow Nulls	
🔑	Pdt_AcctSet_VC	varchar	20		
	Cost_Method_VC	varchar	5		
	Stock_IN	int	4		
	Payable_IN	int	4		
	Shipment_IN	int	4		

Designing Product Account Set Table

The Cost_Method_VC field plays an important role in determining how a product item should be priced, when a product is sold to a customer. At present, we have two alternative in pricing MaxCorp product, the first-in-first-out (FIFO) method and the cost average method. Applying the first method, would price MaxCorp's goods on the oldest price first, as for the latter, at an average price. The quantity and pricing of each product item is referenced to the Stock_Balance Table.

Besides determining the pricing method of its out-going goods, Dave would also want the double-entries to flow into the Journal Table, to record the cost of the out-going goods and the cost of purchasing the goods from its suppliers. To achieve this, we need to assign a default inventory account code to record the cost of in-coming and out-going of each product item. In the Stock_IN field, a clearing account (Payable_IN) would need to be assigned to place its purchase cost temporarily, while awaiting billing from respective supplier and a clearing account (Shipment_IN) is assigned to capture its shipment cost, while pending subsequent billing to its customer.

Enter the following fieldnames, data-type, length, and its Allow Null attributes as shown below:

Product_Category_T

Column Name	Data Type	Length	Allow Nulls
Pdt_Category_VC	varchar	20	
Category_Name_VC	varchar	30	
GL_ID	int	4	

Designing Product Category Table

This table contains three important fields, with the last field requiring Dave, to assign two default account code for effecting the double-entries into the Journal Table, each time a user raises an invoice to its customer. We will assign the field Pdt_Category_VC as the primary key, having reference to the Product Table. Firstly, under each product category, Dave would need to assign a default account code for the cost of goods sold amount, to record the pricing cost of its product, secondly, a default account code to record the sales amount of each invoices raised from the client application. We will illustrate this further, using a case study, as we turn to Chapter 11.

Summary

In this Chapter, we have created five Tables that made up the inventory group, the Product_Table,Product_AccountSet_Table,Product_Category_Table,Stock_Movement_T and the Stock_Balance_Table.

To summaries, in this chapter, we have discussed:

- ➢ How to normalize the inventory table by breaking up into several tables.

- ➢ The purpose of creating GL_ID field in Product Category Table

- ➢ The purpose of creating Stock_IN, Payable_IN and Shipment_IN fields in Product_AccountSet Table

- ➢ The purpose of creating the Stock_Balance Table

- ➢ The purpose of creating the Stock_Movement Table

Chapter 4

Developing the Purchase Table

Purchase Table
	CreditorName_VC
	Product_1_ID
	Product_2_ID
	Unit_Price_IN
	Date_DT

Normalizing Purchase Table

The Purchase table would hold information on product code, supplier name, unit price and the date of purchase, transacted by MaxCorp. As you can see from the above table, the field Product_1_ID and Product_2_ID allows Dave to assign two type of product supplied by each of its supplier, while this might comes useful, but, how about those suppliers that only provide one type of product, the second field, would remain idle, and unpopulated. What if a supplier supply more than 2 types of product? Again, this would result in the inefficient use of storage space. To restructure the design of the above table, we again, would run through the normalization procedure, breaking down the table one at a time.

First Normal Form

As discussed previously, we would need to replace the two product_ID fields with a foreign key, referencing a many-to-many relationship between the Product and the Purchase Table. We will name this field, Pdt_ID_VC, which is a primary key assigned in the Product Table. Now, this table would be able to hold as many types of product that are stored in the Product Table. We would also want to truncate the field Unit_Price off the Purchase Table, as this information has already been created under the Stock Balance Table.

Second Normal Form

We understand that, MaxCorp purchase many types of product from its supplier, assuming, if a supplier supply more than two types of products to MaxCorp, it would have to insert another new records in the Purchase Table, having repeating the supplier name twice. This would result in duplication of information, and to eliminate this, we would have to create a separate table specifically to store information on supplier. Thus, we have to replace the CreditorName_VC field with Cred_ID_VC, and assign this field as a foreign key referencing to the Creditor Table.

Third Normal Form

Notice that the above table, does not have a primary key field, and we know that a primary key should be one that uniquely identify a row of record residing in the Purchase Table. We will assign the purchase invoice number as the primary key, as it holds the key to accessing and identifying each individual records maintained in the Purchase Table. Do not forget, we will also need to create a field to hold the journal number, dictating the double-entries for each purchase transaction.

Enter the above Column names, data type, length and allow null attributes for the Purchase Table, shown below:

Purchase Table

Purchase_T

	Column Name	Data Type	Length	Allow Nulls
	Cred_ID_VC	varchar	20	
	Pdt_ID_VC	varchar	20	✓
	Doc_No_VC	varchar	20	
	Date_DT	datetime	8	
	Status_BT	bit	1	
🔑	Inv_ID_VC	varchar	30	

We will set the fieldname Inv_ID_VC as a primary key, which would be a suitable unique identifier to each individual row of records maintained in the Purchase Table, in our case, we shall insert the purchase invoice number in this field. We will create the Cred_ID_VC field, and assign this field as a foreign key, referencing to the Creditor Table. We have now, established a one-to-many relationship between Purchase Table and Creditor Table, where one creditor may refer to more than one purchase records residing in the Purchase Table. Similarly, we would also want to assign the field Pdt_ID_VC as a foreign key, as one product can have more than one reference to the Purchase Table. We shall include a field to keep track on the payment status of each supplier, with an attribute of 1, denoting a paid status, and 0 for unpaid status.

Designing Creditor Table

Enter the below Column names, data type, length and allow null attributes for the Creditor Table, shown below:

Creditor_T				
	Column Name	Data Type	Length	Allow Nulls
🔑	Cred_ID_VC	varchar	20	
	Cred_Name_VC	varchar	20	
	Cred_Add_VC	varchar	50	✓
	Cred_Contact_VC	varchar	20	✓
	Credit_Term_TI	tinyint	1	
	Cred_Code_IN	int	4	

As mentioned previously, a creditor may have several purchase records residing in the Purchase Table; therefore, we will create a separate table for the supplier of MaxCorp. We set the Cred_ID_VC as the primary key for this table and as a foreign key in the Purchase Table. The fieldname, Credit_Term_TI, would record the credit term, in days given for every purchase made by MaxCorp. This field will hold the key, to calculating the ageing period of each purchase invoice. We shall discuss more on this area, when we move towards Chapter 10. The fieldname Cred_Code_IN allows Dave to assign the default account code for each supplier. This will be useful, when Dave begin to process its suppliers' invoices. As for now, we shall maintain one account code across all suppliers. The amount posted for each invoice will interface with the clearing account, as defined in Product_AccountSet_Table under the fieldname: Payable_TI.

Summary

In Chapter 4, we have learned how to break down the Purchase Table into three separate tables, the Purchase Table, the Product Table and the Creditor Table.

To summaries, in this chapter, we have discussed:

> How to normalize the Purchase Table by breaking up and eliminating some duplicated field.

> The process and motive of creating a separate table for Supplier

> The purpose of creating Credit_Term_TI field in Creditor Table

> The purpose of creating Cred_Code_IN field in Creditor Table

Chapter 5

Developing the Sales Table

```
Sale_T *
   Cust_ID_VC
   Pdt_ID_VC
   Doc_No_VC
   Date_DT
   Status_BT
 🔑 Inv_ID_VC
```

Normalizing Sale Table

In Chapter 2, we have learned how to create Sale Table for MaxCorp, now; it is time to break down this table as we discover more missing elements that we will include in the Sale table, as we progress further from here.

First Normal Form

It is generally logical, to have repeated sale coming from any of MaxCorp's customer, and Dave would need to record the billing transaction details in the Sale Table. Notice, the above table has one field created for each customer, and Dave would have to repeat entering the same customer name again if there is recurring sale coming from the same customer. This would significantly consume a great amount of space, and would definitely slow down the performance of your database server. What we witness here, is duplication of unnecessary information. We can reduce the amount of unnecessary space consumption by restructuring the above Sale Table. We can start, by, replacing the Cust_ID_VC field with an identity fieldname that identify a particular customer name residing in the Customer Table. Before we go into replacing the original field, we need to create a separate Customer Table to store all customer name and details that has trading activity with MaxCorp.

Second Normal Form

Again, the above table would have a field that would be assigned a primary key element, here, we adopt similar concept as what we have achieved in identifying the primary key for the Purchase Table. We will assign the sales invoice number as the default primary key element. Right click on the Inv_ID_VC field, and set it as primary key. We have to link the fieldname Pdt_ID_VC to its primary key, by highlighting the row on the Product Table, left-click on your mouse, while holding it, drag your mouse towards the Sale Table and release.

Third Normal Form

While MaxCorp is cautious in making timely payment to its supplier, it is equally important as well in ensuring that all debts due are collected in time. Currently, MaxCorp do not have field that store credit term allocated for each of its sales transaction, we will create this field to allow the user to keep track on the ageing of all debts due to MaxCorp. We will include this field in the Customer Table.

Enter the above fieldnames, data type, length and the allow nulls attribute in the Sale Table.

Sale Table

	Column Name	Data Type	Length	Allow Nulls	
	Cust_ID_VC	varchar	20		
	Pdt_ID_VC	varchar	20		
	Doc_No_VC	varchar	20		
	Date_DT	datetime	8		
	Status_BT	bit	1		
🔑	Inv_ID_VC	varchar	20		

Sale_T *

As mentioned under the second normal form, we will assign the Inv_ID_VC as the primary key and unique identifier to individual sale record stored in Sale Table. We could keep track on the collection status of each customer's invoices, by setting the Status_BT field as a bit data type, specifying 1 as paid, and 0 as unpaid status.

Enter the below fieldnames, data type, length and the allow nulls attribute in the Customer Table.

Designing Customer Table

Customer_T

	Column Name	Data Type	Length	Allow Nulls	
🔑	Cust_ID_VC	varchar	20		
	Cust_Name_VC	varchar	30		
	Cust_Add_VC	varchar	50	✓	
	Cust_Contact_VC	varchar	20	✓	
	Credit_Term_TI	tinyint	1		
	Cust_Code_VC	varchar	10		

Notice, that, this table has similar attribute as in the Creditor Table. It contains customer details elements, name, address, contact and credit term. The Cust_Code_VC field will hold the user defined account code for capturing the debtor amount in the Journal Table. We could assign a different debtor account code for each customer, but, the code would need to be created in the COA Table beforehand.

Summary

In Chapter 5, we have discovered the key element that makes up the Sale Table, the importance of creating a customer table and the functions of each fields created in the Sale and Customer Table.

To summaries, in this chapter, we have discussed:

➢ How to normalize the Sale Table by breaking up and eliminating some duplicated field.

➢ The purpose of creating a separate table for customer

➢ The purpose of creating Credit_Term_TI field in Customer Table

➢ The purpose of creating Cust_Code_VC field in Customer Table

Chapter 6

Developing the Cash Table

Cash Table
Chq_No_VC
Descrip_VC
Amt_MO
Date_DT

Normalizing Cash Table

The Cash Table would hold information on payment and collection. Dave has mentioned the key elements that he wants, as shown on the Cash Table drawn above. This table looks simple, but beyond its surface, it holds duplicate information, and some key elements are missing. In the following discussion, we will analyze further on how we can reshape the design of the Cash Table that would benefit MaxCorp more in terms of speed and space efficiency.

First Normal Form

We will attempt to filter out duplicated data contained in the Cash Table. The Amt_MO and Date_DT have been created in the Journal Table, thus we can remove these two fields. We can also do away with the Descrip_VC column, as we have included it in the Journal Table too. We will include the Doc_No_VC field in the Cash Table, as this field would allow us access to the three fields that we have removed from the Cash Table.

Second Normal Form

Dave requested, that, he would like to have some cash flow reports generated for MaxCorp. He would like to review reports that cover on MaxCorp's forecast and bank reconciliation. For this special purpose, we will include two additional key fields in the Cash Table, the Cash_Type_VC and the Cash_Category_VC fields. The Cash_Type_VC field will categories the type of expenditure or income arising from MaxCorp payment and collection. The Cash_Category_VC would be the sub category of the main category type created in the Cash_Type_VC. We will discover this in depth, when we go to Chapter 12.

Third Normal Form

We also want to identify the bankers that, are servicing MaxCorp, for this reason, we shall create an identity field for each of MaxCorp's banker. Create a fieldname: Bank_Code_VC, next create a new table called Bank_T, to store the name, address, contact of each of MaxCorp's bankers. We would also want to interface all payment and collection with the Creditor Table and Customer Table, create the two fields named, AR_Code_IN and AP_Code_IN in the Bank Table.

Enter the following column names, data type, length and allow null attributes in the Cash Table as follows:

Cash_T *				
Column Name	Data Type	Length	Allow Nulls	∧
🔑 Doc_No_VC	varchar	20		
Cash_Type_VC	varchar	20		
Cash_Category_VC	varchar	20		
Chq_No_VC	varchar	20		
Bank_Code_VC	varchar	10		
				∨

Cash Table

We have redefined each of the fieldname created in the above Cash Table, with 4 newly created fieldnames. The first field constitutes a primary key field, as this field would hold a row or a set of records of payment or collection contained in the Journal Table, referencing it as a foreign key in the Journal Table. Each time, a payment or collection transaction processing is made, the user, would have to define the type of expenditure or income under the Cash_Type_VC field. We will go deeper on this topic when we begin to create reports for Dave, under Chapter 12.

Enter the following column names, data type, length and allow null attributes in the Bank Table as follows:

Bank_T *				
Column Name	Data Type	Length	Allow Nulls	∧
🔑 Bank_Code_VC	varchar	10		
Bank_Add_VC	varchar	10	✓	
Bank_Contact_VC	varchar	10	✓	
AR_Code_IN	int	4		
AP_Code_IN	int	4		
				∨

Designing Bank Table

Under this table, set the Bank_Code_VC as the primary key field. Next we would want to provide Dave an option, to select the mode of transaction under the cash form screen. Dave would want to have three choice of transaction, first, an option to select a debtor account code, that will interface with the Cust_Code_VC field, created in the Customer_Table for collection transaction, second, to select a creditor account code, to interface with the Cred_Code_IN field located under the Creditor Table for effecting the payment transaction, and, thirdly, an option to select account code from the COA Table for each cash transaction purposes.

Summary

In Chapter 6, we learned, that, brainstorming with the user, would open up some new ideas and requirement, as what Dave have personally shared his special needs of some cash flow reports from the Cash Table. Then, we discovered the need to include some mandatory fields, just to meet Dave's expectation.

To summarize, in this chapter, we have discussed:

➤ How to normalize the Cash Table by breaking up and eliminating some duplicated field.

➤ The purpose of creating Cash_Category_VC field in the Cash Table.

➤ The purpose of creating AR_Code_IN and AP_Code_IN field in Bank Table

Chapter 7

Developing the Asset Table

Asset Table
- FA_Code_VC
- FA_Descrip_VC
- FA_Amt_MO
- Supplier_VC

Normalizing Asset Table

Dave, have requested that MaxCorp, would want to have a master list for all of its existing assets that would contain some relevant information as depicted on the above table. The asset code, to identify the asset physically, their description, amount paid for the asset, and also the name of its provider. It seems, that, we are close to achieving Dave's requirement, by looking at the above four fields. But, we are still far from reaching our goal at this stage of our design. We will detect missing fields and expanding the columns in the asset table, as we progress further in our below discussion.

First Normal Form

Notice the above table, contains a field that store value for each of MaxCorp's asset, in which we want to eliminate from this table. As mentioned, under Chapter 2, we will contain all debit and credit amount in one central table, the Journal Table, in which a set of double-entry are grouped under a journal number located in the Doc_No_VC fields. Thus, we will include the Doc_No_VC field in the asset table, in replace of the fieldname:FA_Amt_MO.

Second Normal Form

Moving forward, it is unlikely that, MaxCorp will purchase its asset from its same source of supplier. We may want to create a separate table to keep the name and addresses of each of its supplier. Wait, we have previously created a table for creditor, so, let's add the fieldname Cred_Code_IN, but, then again, we may even by pass this field, as we can reference to the Creditor Table via the Doc_No_VC field. We will go into this in more detail under Chapter 13, where we will start creating reports from the asset table.

Third Normal Form

Dave has requested that, he would like to see a summary of all MaxCorp's asset, by type, segregated by different category of treatment. In order to achieve this, we need to create the first field, to hold the asset type, and the second field to contain the treatment category. We shall understand this clearly, as we begin developing the relevant report under Chapter 13. Enter the following column names, data type, length and allow null attributes in the Asset Table as follows:

FixedAsset_T *

Column Name	Data Type	Length	Allow Nulls
FA_ID_IN	int	4	
FA_Type_VC	varchar	20	
FA_Category_VC	varchar	20	
FA_Descrip_VC	varchar	50	
Doc_No_VC	varchar	20	

Designing Asset Table

As we can see, from the table above, we have expanded the fields in the asset table, to include one more important field, the Doc_No_VC that would allow user the access to each particular asset's value, date of purchase and its provider name. We can retrieve all this, by joining the following table in our query, Asset table | Journal Table | Purchase Table | Creditor Table. We will discuss this in more detail as we touches on creating reports for Dave in Chapter 13.

Summary

In Chapter 7, we learned that, MaxCorp wants to maintain a master list of all of its existing asset, then we start to create table to store all information related to its assets, and created some additional fields to meet some of Dave's required reports.

To summarize, in this chapter, we have discussed:

➢ How to normalize the Asset Table by creating and eliminating some duplicated field.

➢ The purpose of creating FA_Type_VC field in the Asset Table.

➢ The purpose of creating FA_Category_VC field in the Asset Table.

Chapter 8

Creating Reports from Journals Table

At this stage of our development, we have completed designing the necessary tables for MaxCorp. Let us recap on the topics we have learned, we have learned how we can normalize all the tables that form the structure of an accounting database, by identifying unnecessary fields, eliminating them, and adding some new fields to accommodate some of Dave's requirement. We know that, the Journal Table is the core location of all double-entries transacted by the user, on each of the accounting module, the purpose of modifying, and creating additional fields in Inventory Table, Purchase Table, Sale Table, Cash Table and Asset Table.

We did a good job in helping Dave, creating and designing the database that will eventually form the foundation, in developing the user forms that, would eventually be able to integrate and communicate with our newly designed accounting database. However, how are we to know, that, the structure we have designed, is workable and running? Will our database perform and produce as what we have designed it to be? In order, to find out if there are any flaws in our design, or any missing elements, that, Dave would wanted, in the first place, we have to test the performance of each table we have created, by creating all the accounting reports, that Dave would require, using some raw data as our test data.

Let us begin by discussing on how and what information we need to gather as our test data in testing our first table, the Journal Table. Dave mentioned, that, he want to find out, if the Journal Table we have designed is able to produce the following reports, as below:

1) Trial Balance Listing
2) Income Statement
3) Income Statement by Segment
4) Balance Sheet
5) Transaction Listing

1) Using SQL to produce Trial Balance

Let us open our first table, the COA Table, and enter the following list of information in each of the fields we have created, as detailed below:

GL_ID	GL_Name_VC	BS_Category_VC	Segment_VC	Status_BT
1000	PPE	FA_Cost	NULL	1
1001	Acc_Deprn	FA	NULL	1
2000	Stock	CA	NULL	1
2001	Prov_ Stk_Obsolete	CA	NULL	1
2002	Bank	CA	NULL	1
2003	Debtor	CA	NULL	1
3000	Creditors	CL	NULL	1
4000	Share_Cap	SF	NULL	1
4001	RE b/f	SF	NULL	1
5001	Revenue_Hardware	Rev	BU1	1
5002	Revenue_Software	Rev	BU2	1
6001	Cost_Hardware	Cos	BU1	1
6002	Cost_Software	Cos	BU2	1
7001	Admin & Utility	Otc	BU3	1
7002	Prov-Stk	Otc	BU1	1
8001	Interest from Bank	Oic	BU2	1
9001	Tax	Tax	BU1	1

The Chart of Account (COA) Table will consist all the accounts elements, that the Journal Table, would reference by matching its records with its GL_ID field (foreign key), against the primary field, GL_ID, created in the COA Table, in order to pull the relevant records residing in each of the fields contained in the COA Table. We shall see, what this means, as we go along creating reports from the Journal Table.

Now, let us enter the following records in our Journal Table, so that, we can query the Journal Table.

Doc_No_VC	GL_ID	Amount_NU	Descrip_VC	Date_DT	Period_TI	Year_SI
JV1000	2003	2000	HP Presario-TX 101 P4	5/12/2007	5	2007
JV1000	5001	-2000	HP Presario-TX 101 P4	5/12/2007	5	2007
JV1001	2003	2000	HP Presario-TX 101 P4	8/22/2007	8	2007
JV1001	5001	-2000	HP Presario-TX 101 P4	8/22/2007	8	2007
JV1002	2003	2500	Red Hat-version 2.0	6/3/2007	6	2007
JV1002	5002	-2500	Red Hat-version 2.0	6/3/2007	6	2007
JV1003	2000	300		7/20/2006	7	2006
JV1003	3000	-300	HP Presario-TX 101 P4	7/20/2006	7	2006
JV1004	2000	180		7/20/2006	7	2006
JV1004	3000	-180	HP Presario-TX 101 P4	7/20/2006	7	2006
JV1005	2000	220		7/20/2006	7	2006
JV1005	3000	-220	Red Hat-version 2.0	7/20/2006	7	2006
JV1002	2000	-100	Red Hat-version 2.0	6/3/2007	6	2007
JV1002	6002	100	Red Hat-version 2.0	6/3/2007	6	2007
JV1000	2000	-150	HP Presario-TX 101 P4	5/12/2007	5	2007
JV1000	6001	150	HP Presario-TX 101 P4	5/12/2007	5	2007
JV1001	2000	-150	HP Presario-TX 101 P4	8/22/2007	8	2007
JV1001	6001	150	HP Presario-TX 101 P4	8/22/2007	8	2007
JV1009	2001	-150		12/28/2007	12	2007
JV1009	7002	150		12/28/2007	12	2007
JV1010	1000	600	Purchase OfficeEquip	12/28/2006	12	2006
JV1010	1000	650	Purchase Furniture	12/28/2006	12	2006
JV1010	1000	460	Purchase CompEquip	12/28/2006	12	2006
JV1010	3000	-1710	Purchase FA	12/28/2007	12	2006
JV1011	1000	-60	CE DispCost	7/25/2006	7	2006
JV1011	1000	-100	OE DispCost	7/25/2006	7	2006
JV1011	1000	-100	FF DispCost	7/25/2006	7	2006
JV1011	4001	260	Disposal	7/25/2006	7	2006
JV1011	1001	50	CE DispDeprn	7/25/2006	7	2006
JV1011	1001	100	OE DispDeprn	7/25/2006	7	2006
JV1011	1001	95	FF DispDeprn	7/25/2006	7	2006
JV1011	4001	-245	Disposal	7/25/2006	7	2006
JV1012	1001	-300	CE Deprn	7/25/2006	7	2006
JV1012	1001	-400	OE Deprn	7/25/2006	7	2006
JV1012	1001	-250	FF Deprn	7/25/2006	7	2006
JV1012	4001	950	Deprn	7/25/2006	7	2006
JV1013	1000	800	Purchase CompEquip	2/20/2007	2	2007
JV1013	1000	450	Purchase OfficeEquip	2/20/2007	2	2007
JV1013	1000	360	Purchase Funiture	2/20/2007	2	2007
JV1013	3000	-1610	Purchase FA	2/20/2007	2	2007
JV1014	1001	-200	CE Deprn	12/28/2007	12	2007
JV1014	1001	-120	OE Deprn	12/28/2007	12	2007
JV1014	1001	-55	FF Deprn	12/28/2007	12	2007
JV1014	7001	375	Deprn	12/28/2007	12	2007
JV1015	1000	-50	CE DispCost	6/26/2007	6	2007
JV1015	1000	-100	OE DispCost	6/26/2007	6	2007
JV1015	1000	-10	FF DispCost	6/26/2007	6	2007
JV1015	7001	160	Disposal	6/26/2007	6	2007
JV1016	1001	20	CE DispDeprn	6/26/2007	6	2007
JV1016	1001	55	OE DispDeprn	6/26/2007	6	2007
JV1016	1001	5	FF DispDeprn	6/26/2007	6	2007

JV1016	7001	-80	Disposal	6/26/2007	6	2007
JV1017	7001	745	Payment of interest	12/26/2007	12	2007
JV1017	2002	-745	Payment of interest	12/26/2007	12	2007
JV1018	9001	600	Payment of taxes	7/25/2007	7	2007
JV1018	2002	-600	Payment of taxes	7/25/2007	7	2007
JV1019	2002	250	Interest from bank	7/25/2007	7	2007
JV1019	8001	-250	Interest from bank	7/25/2007	7	2007
JV1020	2002	2000	Proceeds frm shares issue	8/25/2007	8	2007
JV1020	4000	-2000	Proceeds frm shares issue	8/25/2007	8	2007
JV1021	3000	1710	Purchase FA	6/25/2007	6	2007
JV1021	2002	-1710	Purchase FA	6/25/2007	6	2007
JV1022	2002	2000	Receipt frm William	8/26/2007	8	2007
JV1022	2003	-2000	Receipt frm William	8/26/2007	8	2007
JV1023	2002	2000	Receipt frm Randy	8/26/2007	8	2007
JV1023	2003	-2000	Receipt frm Randy	7/23/2007	7	2007

What, a list! Well, this is the first and the last time, we will be capturing such a long list of records, as the following chapter to come, the records we are about to enter is much shorter than the Journal Table. This is what our Journal Table will contain eventually, detailing a list of all the double-entries records, that Dave and its accounting employees have provided as a sample of test data.

Now, open up your SQL Server 2000, click on Tools on the menu bar, and then select SQL Query Analyzer. On the SQL Query Analyzer screen, make sure, you are at the right database mode, if not, select the appropriate database, by clicking on the dropdown list box, and select the right accounting database name, AIS.

Enter the following select query on the blank screen now,

```
select Journal_T.GL_ID as [Acct Code],GL_Name_VC as [Acct Name],
 case when
  sum(case when BS_Category_VC in ('FA_Cost') and Amount_NU > 0 then
  Amount_NU else 0 end) +
  sum(case when BS_Category_VC in ('FA_Cost') and Amount_NU < 0 then
  Amount_NU else 0 end) > 0 then sum(Amount_NU) else 0 end as
  [Debit Bal],
 case when
  sum(case when BS_Category_VC in ('FA_Cost') and Amount_NU > 0 then
  Amount_NU else 0 end) +
  sum(case when BS_Category_VC in ('FA_Cost') and Amount_NU < 0 then
  Amount_NU else 0 end) < 0  then sum(Amount_NU) else 0 end as
  [Credit Bal]

from Journal_T join COA_T
on Journal_T.GL_ID = COA_T.GL_ID
where BS_Category_VC in ('FA_Cost')
group by GL_Name_VC,Journal_T.GL_ID

union all
```

```sql
select Journal_T.GL_ID as [Acct Code],GL_Name_VC as [Acct Name],
 case when
  sum(case when BS_Category_VC in ('FA') and Amount_NU > 0 then
  Amount_NU else 0 end) +
  sum(case when BS_Category_VC in ('FA') and Amount_NU < 0 then
  Amount_NU else 0 end) > 0
  then sum(Amount_NU) else 0 end as [Debit Bal],
 case when
  sum(case when BS_Category_VC in ('FA') and Amount_NU > 0 then
  Amount_NU else 0 end) +
  sum(case when BS_Category_VC in ('FA') and Amount_NU < 0 then
  Amount_NU else 0 end) < 0
  then sum(Amount_NU) else 0 end as [Credit Bal]

from Journal_T join COA_T
on Journal_T.GL_ID = COA_T.GL_ID
where BS_Category_VC in ('FA')
group by GL_Name_VC,Journal_T.GL_ID

union all

select Journal_T.GL_ID as [Acct Code],GL_Name_VC as [Acct Name],
 case when
  sum(case when BS_Category_VC in ('CA') and Amount_NU > 0 then
  Amount_NU else 0 end) +
  sum(case when BS_Category_VC in ('CA') and Amount_NU < 0 then
  Amount_NU else 0 end) > 0
  then sum(Amount_NU) else 0 end as [Debit Bal],
 case when
  sum(case when BS_Category_VC in ('CA') and Amount_NU > 0 then
  Amount_NU else 0 end) +
  sum(case when BS_Category_VC in ('CA') and Amount_NU < 0 then
  Amount_NU else 0 end) < 0
  then sum(Amount_NU) else 0 end as [Credit Bal]

from Journal_T join COA_T
on Journal_T.GL_ID = COA_T.GL_ID
where BS_Category_VC in ('CA')
group by GL_Name_VC,Journal_T.GL_ID

union all

select Journal_T.GL_ID as [Acct Code],GL_Name_VC as [Acct Name],
 case when
  sum(case when BS_Category_VC in ('CL') and Amount_NU > 0 then
  Amount_NU else 0 end) +
  sum(case when BS_Category_VC in ('CL') and Amount_NU < 0 then
  Amount_NU else 0 end) > 0

  then sum(Amount_NU) else 0 end as [Debit Bal],
 case when
  sum(case when BS_Category_VC in ('CL') and Amount_NU > 0 then
```

```
   Amount_NU else 0 end) +
   sum(case when BS_Category_VC in ('CL') and Amount_NU < 0 then
   Amount_NU else 0 end) < 0
   then sum(Amount_NU) else 0 end as [Credit Bal]

from Journal_T join COA_T
on Journal_T.GL_ID = COA_T.GL_ID
where BS_Category_VC in ('CL')
group by GL_Name_VC,Journal_T.GL_ID

union all

select Journal_T.GL_ID as [Acct Code],GL_Name_VC as [Acct Name],
 case when
   sum(case when BS_Category_VC in ('SF') and Amount_NU > 0 then
   Amount_NU else 0 end) +
   sum(case when BS_Category_VC in ('SF') and Amount_NU < 0 then
   Amount_NU else 0 end) > 0
   then sum(Amount_NU) else 0 end as [Debit Bal],
 case when
   sum(case when BS_Category_VC in ('SF') and Amount_NU > 0 then
   Amount_NU else 0 end) +
   sum(case when BS_Category_VC in ('SF') and Amount_NU < 0 then
   Amount_NU else 0 end) < 0
   then sum(Amount_NU) else 0 end as [Credit Bal]

from Journal_T join COA_T
on Journal_T.GL_ID = COA_T.GL_ID
where BS_Category_VC in ('SF')
group by GL_Name_VC,Journal_T.GL_ID

union all

select Journal_T.GL_ID as [Acct Code],GL_Name_VC as [Acct Name],
 case when
   sum(case when BS_Category_VC in ('Rev') and Year_SI = 2007 and
   Amount_NU < 0 then Amount_NU else 0 end) +
   sum(case when BS_Category_VC in ('Rev') and Year_SI = 2007 and
   Amount_NU > 0 then Amount_NU else 0 end) > 0
   then sum(Amount_NU) else 0 end as [Debit Bal],
 case when
   sum(case when BS_Category_VC in ('Rev') and Year_SI = 2007 and
   Amount_NU < 0 then Amount_NU else 0 end) +
   sum(case when BS_Category_VC in ('Rev') and Year_SI = 2007 and
   Amount_NU > 0 then Amount_NU else 0 end) < 0
   then sum(Amount_NU) else 0 end as [Credit Bal]

from Journal_T join COA_T
on Journal_T.GL_ID = COA_T.GL_ID
where BS_Category_VC in ('Rev')
group by GL_Name_VC,Journal_T.GL_ID
```

```
union all

select Journal_T.GL_ID as [Acct Code],GL_Name_VC as [Acct Name],
 case when
  sum(case when BS_Category_VC in ('Cos') and Year_SI = 2007 and
  Amount_NU > 0 then Amount_NU else 0 end) +
  sum(case when BS_Category_VC in ('Cos') and Year_SI = 2007 and
  Amount_NU < 0 then Amount_NU else 0 end) > 0
  then sum(Amount_NU) else 0 end as [Debit Bal],

 case when
  sum(case when BS_Category_VC in ('Cos') and Year_SI = 2007 and
  Amount_NU > 0 then Amount_NU else 0 end) +
  sum(case when BS_Category_VC in ('Cos') and Year_SI = 2007 and
  Amount_NU < 0 then Amount_NU else 0 end) < 0
  then sum(Amount_NU) else 0 end as [Credit Bal]

from Journal_T join COA_T
on Journal_T.GL_ID = COA_T.GL_ID
where BS_Category_VC in ('Cos')
group by GL_Name_VC,Journal_T.GL_ID

union all

select Journal_T.GL_ID as [Acct Code],GL_Name_VC as [Acct Name],
 case when
  sum(case when BS_Category_VC in ('Otc') and Year_SI = 2007 and
  Amount_NU > 0 then Amount_NU else 0 end) +
  sum(case when BS_Category_VC in ('Otc') and Year_SI = 2007 and
  Amount_NU < 0 then Amount_NU else 0 end) > 0
  then sum(Amount_NU) else 0 end as [Debit Bal],
 case when
  sum(case when BS_Category_VC in ('Otc') and Year_SI = 2007 and
  Amount_NU > 0 then Amount_NU else 0 end) +
  sum(case when BS_Category_VC in ('Otc') and Year_SI = 2007 and
  Amount_NU < 0 then Amount_NU else 0 end) < 0
  then sum(Amount_NU) else 0 end as [Credit Bal]

from Journal_T join COA_T
on Journal_T.GL_ID = COA_T.GL_ID
where BS_Category_VC in ('Otc')
group by GL_Name_VC,Journal_T.GL_ID

union all

select Journal_T.GL_ID as [Acct Code],GL_Name_VC as [Acct Name],
 case when
  sum(case when BS_Category_VC in ('Oic') and Year_SI = 2007 and
  Amount_NU < 0 then Amount_NU else 0 end) +
  sum(case when BS_Category_VC in ('Oic') and Year_SI = 2007 and
  Amount_NU > 0 then Amount_NU else 0 end) > 0
  then sum(Amount_NU) else 0 end as [Debit Bal],
```

```
case when
  sum(case when BS_Category_VC in ('Oic') and Year_SI = 2007 and
  Amount_NU < 0 then Amount_NU else 0 end) +
  sum(case when BS_Category_VC in ('Oic') and Year_SI = 2007 and
  Amount_NU > 0 then Amount_NU else 0 end) < 0
  then sum(Amount_NU) else 0 end as [Credit Bal]

from Journal_T join COA_T
on Journal_T.GL_ID = COA_T.GL_ID
where BS_Category_VC in ('Oic')
group by GL_Name_VC,Journal_T.GL_ID

union all

select Journal_T.GL_ID as [Acct Code],GL_Name_VC as [Acct Name],
 case when
  sum(case when BS_Category_VC in ('Tax') and Year_SI = 2007 and
  Amount_NU > 0 then Amount_NU else 0 end) +
  sum(case when BS_Category_VC in ('Tax') and Year_SI = 2007 and
  Amount_NU < 0 then Amount_NU else 0 end) > 0
  then sum(Amount_NU) else 0 end as [Debit Bal],
 case when
  sum(case when BS_Category_VC in ('Tax') and Year_SI = 2007 and
  Amount_NU > 0 then Amount_NU else 0 end) +
  sum(case when BS_Category_VC in ('Tax') and Year_SI = 2007 and
  Amount_NU < 0 then Amount_NU else 0 end) < 0
  then sum(Amount_NU) else 0 end as [Credit Bal]

from Journal_T join COA_T
on Journal_T.GL_ID = COA_T.GL_ID
where BS_Category_VC in ('Tax')
group by GL_Name_VC,Journal_T.GL_ID

union all

select '','Total BS Movement in YR 2007',
 sum( case when Amount_NU >0 and BS_Category_VC in
 ('FA_Cost','FA','CA','CL','SF') then Amount_NU else 0 end) +
 sum( case when Amount_NU <0 and BS_Category_VC in
 ('FA_Cost','FA','CA','CL','SF') then Amount_NU else 0 end),0

from Journal_T join COA_T
on Journal_T.GL_ID = COA_T.GL_ID

union all

select '','Total PL Movement in YR 2007',
 sum( case when Amount_NU <0 and Year_SI = '2007' and BS_Category_VC
in
 ('Rev','Cos','Otc','Oic','Tax') then Amount_NU else 0 end) +
 sum( case when Amount_NU >0 and Year_SI = '2007' and BS_Category_VC
in
```

```
('Rev','Cos','Otc','Oic','Tax') then Amount_NU else 0 end),0
```

```
from Journal_T join COA_T
on Journal_T.GL_ID = COA_T.GL_ID
```

Now, Test your query, by clicking on the parse query button to check for any syntax error, if your syntax is working, you would see the message "The command(s) completed successfully." If not, go through the code above again, and run the parse query until your syntax is working properly. Then, execute the query, by clicking on the execute query button, and you would see the following result.

	Acct Code	Acct Name	Debit Bal	Credit Bal
1	1000	PPE	2900	0
2	1001	Acc_Deprn	0	-1000
3	2000	Stock	300	0
4	2001	Prov_Stk_Obsolete	0	-150
5	2002	Bank	3195	0
6	2003	Debtor	2500	0
7	3000	Creditors	0	-2310
8	4000	Share_Cap	0	-2000
9	4001	RE b/f	965	0
10	5001	Revenue_Hardware	0	-4000
11	5002	Revenue_Software	0	-2500
12	6001	Cost_Hardware	300	0
13	6002	Cost_Software	100	0
14	7001	Admin & Utility	1200	0
15	7002	Prov-Stk	150	0
16	8001	Interest from Bank	0	-250
17	9001	Tax	600	0
18	0	Total BS Movement in YR 2007	4400	0
19	0	Total PL Movement in YR 2007	-4400	0

We have finally produced our first report for Dave, the Trial Balance listing. Notice, the last two row, reflecting a positive and a negative figure of 4400, this serve as a check point, where it tells Dave, that the accounts produce a profit of $4,400, reconcilable to the net movement in income statement, and balance sheet in year 2007. Notice the query above, consist of a few select query that are joined together, using the union all clause. The list of the accounts code, name and amount is properly arranged in ascending order, by account code, exactly as how we have typed in our sql syntax.

Let us go through the function of the above select query which we have successfully completed.

How It Works – Select Query for Trial Balance Listing

Now, let us break up our code into two section, the first section, will explain how we identify an income or expense, in other words, profit or loss elements, their positive or negative amount, and then, how we should place the amount on the trial balance listing. Next, we identify how the balance sheet elements are extracted and populated on the trial balance listing.

Let us take our first code, identifying the income or expense elements,

```
select Journal_T.GL_ID as [Acct Code],GL_Name_VC as [Acct Name],
 case when
  sum(case when BS_Category_VC in ('Rev') and Year_SI = 2007 and
  Amount_NU < 0 then Amount_NU else 0 end) +
  sum(case when BS_Category_VC in ('Rev') and Year_SI = 2007 and
  Amount_NU > 0 then Amount_NU else 0 end) > 0
  then sum(Amount_NU) else 0 end as [Debit Bal],
```

Here, we select our first column, the account code from the Journal Table, assigning an alias name of "Acct Code", and then we select our second column, the account name, giving an alias name of "Acct Name". Next, we sum up the value of those records, that are categorized as 'Rev', in the year '2007', with positive and negative amount, if the summed amount is greater then 0, then we place it on the third column, named "Debit Bal".

Likewise, if the summed amount is lesser than 0, then it should be placed on the fourth column, called "Credit Bal".

```
case when
  sum(case when BS_Category_VC in ('Rev') and Year_SI = 2007 and
  Amount_NU < 0 then Amount_NU else 0 end) +
  sum(case when BS_Category_VC in ('Rev') and Year_SI = 2007 and
  Amount_NU > 0 then Amount_NU else 0 end) < 0
  then sum(Amount_NU) else 0 end as [Credit Bal]
```

Remember, our first and second selection, on the account code and name, we just want those records categorized as "Rev" only. We join both the Journal Table and COA Table, in order for us to filter the category field, to pull only those accounts name categorized as "Rev" to appear on the Trial Balance listing.

```
from Journal_T join COA_T
on Journal_T.GL_ID = COA_T.GL_ID
where BS_Category_VC in ('Rev')
group by GL_Name_VC,Journal_T.GL_ID
```

Next, we analyse our select query on the balance sheet section,

```
select Journal_T.GL_ID as [Acct Code],GL_Name_VC as [Acct Name],
 case when
  sum(case when BS_Category_VC in ('CA') and Amount_NU > 0 then
  Amount_NU else 0 end) +
  sum(case when BS_Category_VC in ('CA') and Amount_NU < 0 then
  Amount_NU else 0 end) > 0
  then sum(Amount_NU) else 0 end as [Debit Bal],
```

Here, the select query is the same as the one we have analyzed previously. The only difference in this section code is we are filtering the balance sheet element, applying the same filtering condition, locating those records with the "CA" category. We then place the summed amount on the third column, if greater than 0.

Similarly, we then place the summed amount on the fourth column, if lesser than 0.

```
case when
  sum(case when BS_Category_VC in ('CA') and Amount_NU > 0 then
  Amount_NU else 0 end) +
  sum(case when BS_Category_VC in ('CA') and Amount_NU < 0 then
  Amount_NU else 0 end) < 0
  then sum(Amount_NU) else 0 end as [Credit Bal]
```

Next, we join the Journal Table and the COA Table, so that we can filter those account codes and its corresponding name, having categorized as "CA", by referencing each records in the Journal Table to those residing in the COA Table.

```
from Journal_T join COA_T
on Journal_T.GL_ID = COA_T.GL_ID
where BS_Category_VC in ('CA')
group by GL_Name_VC,Journal_T.GL_ID
```

2) Using SQL to produce Income Statement

This report, generally show how well, MaxCorp's trading is performing. Is MaxCorp, generating profit, or a loss? We shall see when we begin to create and then run our select query for the income statement.

Enter the following select query on the blank screen dialog box appearing on your SQL Query Analyzer:

```
select Journal_T.GL_ID as [Acct Code],GL_Name_VC as
 [Revenue],sum(Amount_NU) as [YTD]
 from Journal_T join COA_T

on Journal_T.GL_ID = COA_T.GL_ID
```

```sql
where Year_SI = 2007
and BS_Category_VC ='Rev'
GROUP by GL_Name_VC,Journal_T.GL_ID

union all

select 0, 'Total Revenue',sum(Amount_NU)

from Journal_T join COA_T
on Journal_T.GL_ID = COA_T.GL_ID
where Year_SI = 2007
and BS_Category_VC = 'Rev'

select Journal_T.GL_ID as [Acct Code],GL_Name_VC as [Cost of Sales],
 sum(Amount_NU)as [YTD]

from Journal_T join COA_T
on Journal_T.GL_ID = COA_T.GL_ID
where Year_SI = 2007
and BS_Category_VC = 'Cos'
GROUP by GL_Name_VC,Journal_T.GL_ID

union all

select 0, 'Total Cost of Sales',sum(Amount_NU) as [YTD]

from Journal_T join COA_T
on Journal_T.GL_ID = COA_T.GL_ID
where Year_SI = 2007
and BS_Category_VC = 'Cos'

union all

select 0,'Gross Profit',
 sum(case  when  Year_SI = 2007  and  BS_Category_VC  =  'Rev'  then
Amount_NU
 else 0 end)+
 sum(case  when  Year_SI = 2007  and  BS_Category_VC  =  'Cos'  then
Amount_NU
 else 0 end)AS [YTD]

from Journal_T join COA_T
on Journal_T.GL_ID = COA_T.GL_ID

select  Journal_T.GL_ID  as  [Acct  Code],GL_Name_VC  as  [Less  Other
Cost], sum(Amount_NU)as [YTD]
from Journal_T join COA_T
on Journal_T.GL_ID = COA_T.GL_ID
where Year_SI = 2007
and BS_Category_VC = 'Otc'
GROUP by Journal_T.GL_ID,GL_Name_VC
```

```sql
union all

select 0, 'Total Other Cost',sum(Amount_NU) as [YTD]

from Journal_T join COA_T
on Journal_T.GL_ID = COA_T.GL_ID
where Year_SI = 2007
and BS_Category_VC = 'Otc'

select  Journal_T.GL_ID  as  [Acct  Code],GL_Name_VC  as  [Add  Other
Income], sum(Amount_NU)as [YTD]

from Journal_T join COA_T
on Journal_T.GL_ID = COA_T.GL_ID
where Year_SI = 2007
and BS_Category_VC = 'Oic'
GROUP by Journal_T.GL_ID,GL_Name_VC

union all

select 0, 'Total Other Income',sum(Amount_NU) as [YTD]

from Journal_T join COA_T
on Journal_T.GL_ID = COA_T.GL_ID
where Year_SI = 2007
and BS_Category_VC = 'Oic'

union all

select 0, 'Total Operating Cost/Income',
 sum(case  when  Year_SI  =  2007  and  BS_Category_VC  =  'Otc'  then
Amount_NU else 0 end)+
 sum(case  when  Year_SI  =  2007  and  BS_Category_VC  =  'Oic'  then
Amount_NU else 0 end)

from Journal_T join COA_T
on Journal_T.GL_ID = COA_T.GL_ID

union all

select 0, 'Profit Before Tax (PBT)',
 sum(case  when  Year_SI  =  2007  and  BS_Category_VC  =  'Rev'  then
Amount_NU else 0 end)+
 sum(case  when  Year_SI  =  2007  and  BS_Category_VC  =  'Cos'  then
Amount_NU else 0 end)+
 sum(case  when  Year_SI  =  2007  and  BS_Category_VC  =  'Otc'  then
Amount_NU else 0 end)+
 sum(case  when  Year_SI  =  2007  and  BS_Category_VC  =  'Oic'  then
Amount_NU else 0 end)

from Journal_T join COA_T
on Journal_T.GL_ID = COA_T.GL_ID
```

```
select Journal_T.GL_ID as [Acct Code],GL_Name_VC as [Income Tax],
 sum(Amount_NU)as [YTD]

from Journal_T join COA_T
on Journal_T.GL_ID = COA_T.GL_ID
where Year_SI = 2007
and BS_Category_VC = 'Tax'
GROUP by Journal_T.GL_ID,GL_Name_VC

union all

select 0, 'Profit After Tax (PAT)',
 sum(case  when  Year_SI  =  2007  and  BS_Category_VC  =  'Rev'  then
Amount_NU else 0 end)+
 sum(case  when  Year_SI  =  2007  and  BS_Category_VC  =  'Cos'  then
Amount_NU else 0 end)+
 sum(case  when  Year_SI  =  2007  and  BS_Category_VC  =  'Otc'  then
Amount_NU else 0 end)+
 sum(case  when  Year_SI  =  2007  and  BS_Category_VC  =  'Oic'  then
Amount_NU else 0 end)+
 sum(case  when  Year_SI  =  2007  and  BS_Category_VC  =  'Tax'  then
Amount_NU else 0 end)

from Journal_T join COA_T
on Journal_T.GL_ID = COA_T.GL_ID
```

Now, Test your query, by clicking on the parse query button to check for any syntax error, if your syntax is working, you would see the message "The command(s) completed successfully." If not, go through the code above again, and run the parse query until your syntax is working properly. Then, execute the query, by clicking on the execute query button, you would see the following on your result pane below.

	Acct Code	Revenue	YTD
1	5001	Revenue_Hardware	-4000
2	5002	Revenue_Software	-2500
3	0	Total Revenue	-6500

	Acct Code	Cost of Sales	YTD
1	6001	Cost_Hardware	300
2	6002	Cost_Software	100
3	0	Total Cost of Sales	400
4	0	Gross Profit	-6100

	Acct Code	Less Other Cost	YTD
1	7001	Admin & Utility	1200
2	7002	Prov-Stk	150
3	0	Total Other Cost	1350

	Acct Code	Add Other Income	YTD
1	8001	Interest from Bank	-250
2	0	Total Other Income	-250
3	0	Total Operating Cost/Income	1100
4	0	Profit Before Tax (PBT)	-5000

	Acct Code	Income Tax	YTD
1	9001	Tax	600
2	0	Profit After Tax (PAT)	-4400

Grids Messages

Notice, the above result, shows that, MaxCorp, has made a profit after tax of $4,400, which is the exact amount shown on the face of our Trial Balance listing as the net movement in income statement and balance sheet. We have four blocks that form a complete income statement, beginning with the Revenue section; the cost of goods sold section, other cost and other income sections. We shall see further, how our select query works and produce what we have wanted.

How it Works – Select Query for Income Statement

Our first section code has similar function as what we have gone through in creating the select query for the trial balance listing. We first, select the account code to be our first column, next, the account name, assigning an alias of "Revenue", we then sum the amount of all the records having categorized as "Rev" created in year "2007", using the where clause. We then group our result, first, by the account name, next by account code.

```
select Journal_T.GL_ID as [Acct Code],GL_Name_VC as
 [Revenue],sum(Amount_NU) as [YTD]

 from Journal_T join COA_T

on Journal_T.GL_ID = COA_T.GL_ID
where Year_SI = 2007
and BS_Category_VC ='Rev'
group by GL_Name_VC,Journal_T.GL_ID
```

We then, create a row for totaling up the Revenue amount, having joined with the above result, appearing as a subtotal for the revenue amount, using the union all clause to combine the two queries. Notice that, our first select is 0, as this is merely a formatting preference, we need to have an equal number of queries in order for the union all operators to function properly, you can include other phrase as you may prefer. Again, we join the Journal Table with the COA Table together, so that, we can only extract those records that have the category attribute of "Rev" assigned and with the Year attribute of "2007".

```
union all

select 0, 'Total Revenue',sum(Amount_NU) from Journal_T join COA_T
on Journal_T.GL_ID = COA_T.GL_ID
where Year_SI = 2007
and BS_Category_VC = 'Rev'
```

The rest of the select query will perform the same function, as we only, need to replace the current category attribute with the remaining category as contained in the COA Table.

On our last section of the select query, we compute the profit after tax, by summing up the entire category, having the 2007 year attribute only.

```
select 0, 'Profit After Tax (PAT)',
 sum(case  when  Year_SI  =  2007  and  BS_Category_VC  =  'Rev'  then
Amount_NU else 0 end)+
 sum(case  when  Year_SI  =  2007  and  BS_Category_VC  =  'Cos'  then
Amount_NU else 0 end)+
 sum(case  when  Year_SI  =  2007  and  BS_Category_VC  -  'Otc'  then
Amount_NU else 0 end)+
 sum(case  when  Year_SI  =  2007  and  BS_Category_VC  =  'Oic'  then
Amount_NU else 0 end)+
 sum(case  when  Year_SI  =  2007  and  BS_Category_VC  =  'Tax'  then
Amount_NU else 0 end)
```

```
from Journal_T join COA_T
on Journal_T.GL_ID = COA_T.GL_ID
```

3) Using SQL to produce Income Statement by Segment

Dave has mentioned, in Chapter 2, that MaxCorp's trading performance would be measured on a group of business units. Let us create another set of select query that would show the income statement by segment.

Enter the following select query now,

```
select Journal_T.GL_ID as [Acct Code], GL_Name_VC as [Revenue],
 sum(case when Year_SI = 2007 and BS_Category_VC = 'Rev' and
 Segment_VC = 'BU1' then Amount_NU else 0 end) as [BU1],
 sum(case when Year_SI = 2007 and BS_Category_VC = 'Rev' and
 Segment_VC = 'BU2' then Amount_NU else 0 end) as [BU2],
 sum(case when Year_SI = 2007 and BS_Category_VC = 'Rev' and
 Segment_VC = 'BU3' then Amount_NU else 0 end) as [BU3],
 sum(case when Year_SI = 2007 then Amount_NU else 0 end)
 as [Year to Date]

from Journal_T join COA_T
on Journal_T.GL_ID = COA_T.GL_ID
where BS_Category_VC = 'Rev'
group by GL_Name_VC,Journal_T.GL_ID

union all

select 0 ,'Total Revenue',
 sum(case when Year_SI = 2007 and BS_Category_VC = 'Rev' and
 Segment_VC = 'BU1' then Amount_NU else 0 end) as [BU1],
 sum(case when Year_SI = 2007 and BS_Category_VC = 'Rev' and
 Segment_VC = 'BU2' then Amount_NU else 0 end) as [BU2],
 sum(case when Year_SI = 2007 and BS_Category_VC = 'Rev' and
 Segment_VC = 'BU3' then Amount_NU else 0 end) as [BU3],
 sum(case when Year_SI = 2007 and BS_Category_VC = 'Rev' then
 Amount_NU else 0 end) as [Year to Date]

from Journal_T join COA_T
on Journal_T.GL_ID = COA_T.GL_ID

select  Journal_T.GL_ID  as  [Acct  Code],  GL_Name_VC  as  [Cost  of
Sales],
 sum(case when Year_SI = 2007 and BS_Category_VC = 'Cos' and
 Segment_VC = 'BU1' then Amount_NU else 0 end) as [BU1],
 sum(case when Year_SI = 2007 and BS_Category_VC = 'Cos' and
 Segment_VC = 'BU2' then Amount_NU else 0 end) as [BU2],
 sum(case when Year_SI = 2007 and BS_Category_VC = 'Cos' and
 Segment_VC = 'BU3' then Amount_NU else 0 end) as [BU3],
```

```sql
 sum(case when Year_SI = 2007 then Amount_NU else 0 end)
 as [Year to Date]

from Journal_T join COA_T
on Journal_T.GL_ID = COA_T.GL_ID
where BS_Category_VC = 'Cos'
group by GL_Name_VC,Journal_T.GL_ID

union all

select 0 ,'Total Cost of Sales',
 sum(case when Year_SI = 2007 and BS_Category_VC = 'Cos' and
 Segment_VC = 'BU1' then Amount_NU else 0 end) as [BU1],
 sum(case when Year_SI = 2007 and BS_Category_VC = 'Cos' and
 Segment_VC = 'BU2' then Amount_NU else 0 end) as [BU2],
 sum(case when Year_SI = 2007 and BS_Category_VC = 'Cos' and
 Segment_VC = 'BU3' then Amount_NU else 0 end) as [BU3],
 sum(case when Year_SI = 2007 and BS_Category_VC = 'Cos' then
 Amount_NU else 0 end) as [Year to Date]

from Journal_T join COA_T
on Journal_T.GL_ID = COA_T.GL_ID

union all

select 0,'Gross Profit',
 sum(case when Year_SI = 2007 and BS_Category_VC = 'Rev' and
 Segment_VC = 'BU1' then Amount_NU else 0 end)+
 sum(case when Year_SI = 2007 and BS_Category_VC = 'Cos' and
 Segment_VC = 'BU1' then Amount_NU else 0 end)as [BU1],
 sum(case when Year_SI = 2007 and BS_Category_VC = 'Rev' and
 Segment_VC = 'BU2' then Amount_NU else 0 end)+
 sum(case when Year_SI = 2007 and BS_Category_VC = 'Cos' and
 Segment_VC = 'BU2' then Amount_NU else 0 end)as [BU2],
 sum(case when Year_SI = 2007 and BS_Category_VC = 'Rev' and
 Segment_VC = 'BU3' then Amount_NU else 0 end)+
 sum(case when Year_SI = 2007 and BS_Category_VC = 'Cos' and
 Segment_VC = 'BU3' then Amount_NU else 0 end)as [BU3],
 sum(case when Year_SI = 2007 and BS_Category_VC in ('Rev','Cos')
 then Amount_NU else 0 end)as [Year to Date]

from Journal_T join COA_T
on Journal_T.GL_ID = COA_T.GL_ID

select Journal_T.GL_ID as [Acct Code], GL_Name_VC as [Less Other
Cost],
 sum(case when Year_SI = 2007 and BS_Category_VC = 'Otc' and
 Segment_VC = 'BU1' then Amount_NU else 0 end) as [BU1],
 sum(case when Year_SI = 2007 and BS_Category_VC = 'Otc' and
 Segment_VC = 'BU2' then Amount_NU else 0 end) as [BU2],
 sum(case when Year_SI = 2007 and BS_Category_VC = 'Otc' and
 Segment_VC = 'BU3' then Amount_NU else 0 end) as [BU3],
```

```
 sum(case when Year_SI = 2007 then Amount_NU else 0 end)
 as [Year to Date]

from Journal_T join COA_T
on Journal_T.GL_ID = COA_T.GL_ID
where BS_Category_VC = 'Otc'
group by GL_Name_VC,Journal_T.GL_ID

union all

select 0 ,'Total Other Cost',
 sum(case when Year_SI = 2007 and BS_Category_VC = 'Otc' and
 Segment_VC = 'BU1' then Amount_NU else 0 end) as [BU1],
 sum(case when Year_SI = 2007 and BS_Category_VC = 'Otc' and
 Segment_VC = 'BU2' then Amount_NU else 0 end) as [BU2],
 sum(case when Year_SI = 2007 and BS_Category_VC = 'Otc' and
 Segment_VC = 'BU3' then Amount_NU else 0 end) as [BU3],
 sum(case when Year_SI = 2007 then Amount_NU else 0 end)
 as [Year to Date]

from Journal_T join COA_T
on Journal_T.GL_ID = COA_T.GL_ID
where BS_Category_VC = 'Otc'

select Journal_T.GL_ID as [Acct Code], GL_Name_VC
 as [Add Other Income],
 sum(case when Year_SI = 2007 and BS_Category_VC = 'Oic' and
 Segment_VC = 'BU1' then Amount_NU else 0 end) as [BU1],
 sum(case when Year_SI = 2007 and BS_Category_VC = 'Oic' and
 Segment_VC = 'BU2' then Amount_NU else 0 end) as [BU2],
 sum(case when Year_SI = 2007 and BS_Category_VC = 'Oic' and
 Segment_VC = 'BU3' then Amount_NU else 0 end) as [BU3],
 sum(case when Year_SI = 2007 then Amount_NU else 0 end)
 as [Year to Date]

from Journal_T join COA_T
on Journal_T.GL_ID = COA_T.GL_ID
where BS_Category_VC = 'Oic'
group by GL_Name_VC,Journal_T.GL_ID

union all

select 0 ,'Total Other Income',
 sum(case when Year_SI = 2007 and BS_Category_VC = 'Oic' and
 Segment_VC = 'BU1' then Amount_NU else 0 end) as [BU1],
 sum(case when Year_SI = 2007 and BS_Category_VC = 'Oic' and
 Segment_VC = 'BU2' then Amount_NU else 0 end) as [BU2],
 sum(case when Year_SI = 2007 and BS_Category_VC = 'Oic' and
 Segment_VC = 'BU3' then Amount_NU else 0 end) as [BU3],
 sum(case when Year_SI = 2007 then Amount_NU else 0 end)
 as [Year to Date]
```

```sql
from Journal_T join COA_T
on Journal_T.GL_ID = COA_T.GL_ID
where BS_Category_VC = 'Oic'

union all

select 0,'Total Operating Cost/Income',
 sum(case when Year_SI = 2007 and BS_Category_VC in ('Otc','Oic')
and Segment_VC = 'BU1' then Amount_NU else 0 end),
 sum(case when Year_SI = 2007 and BS_Category_VC in ('Otc','Oic')
and Segment_VC = 'BU2' then Amount_NU else 0 end),
 sum(case when Year_SI = 2007 and BS_Category_VC in ('Otc','Oic')
and Segment_VC = 'BU3' then Amount_NU else 0 end),
 sum(case when Year_SI = 2007 and BS_Category_VC in ('Otc','Oic')
then Amount_NU else 0 end)as [Year to Date]

from Journal_T join COA_T
on Journal_T.GL_ID = COA_T.GL_ID

union all

select 0, 'Profit Before Tax (PBT)',
 sum(case when Year_SI = 2007 and
 BS_Category_VC in ('Rev','Cos','Otc','Oic') and
 Segment_VC = 'BU1' then Amount_NU else 0 end),
 sum(case when Year_SI = 2007 and
 BS_Category_VC in ('Rev','Cos','Otc','Oic') and
 Segment_VC = 'BU2' then Amount_NU else 0 end),
 sum(case when Year_SI = 2007 and
 BS_Category_VC in ('Rev','Cos','Otc','Oic') and
 Segment_VC = 'BU3' then Amount_NU else 0 end),
 sum(case when Year_SI = 2007 and
 BS_Category_VC in ('Rev','Cos','Otc','Oic')
 then Amount_NU else 0 end)as [Year to Date]

from Journal_T join COA_T
on Journal_T.GL_ID = COA_T.GL_ID

union all

select Journal_T.GL_ID as [Acct Code], GL_Name_VC as [Income Tax],
 sum(case when Year_SI = 2007 and BS_Category_VC = 'Tax' and
 Segment_VC = 'BU1' then Amount_NU else 0 end) as [BU1],
 sum(case when Year_SI = 2007 and BS_Category_VC = 'Tax' and
 Segment_VC = 'BU2' then Amount_NU else 0 end) as [BU2],
 sum(case when Year_SI = 2007 and BS_Category_VC = 'Tax' and
 Segment_VC = 'BU3' then Amount_NU else 0 end) as [BU3],
 sum(case when Year_SI = 2007 then Amount_NU else 0 end)
 as [Year to Date]

from Journal_T join COA_T
on Journal_T.GL_ID = COA_T.GL_ID
```

```
where BS_Category_VC = 'Tax'
group by GL_Name_VC,Journal_T.GL_ID

union all

select 0, 'Profit After Tax (PAT)',
 sum(case when Year_SI = 2007 and
 BS_Category_VC in ('Rev','Cos','Otc','Oic','Tax') and
 Segment_VC = 'BU1' then Amount_NU else 0 end),
 sum(case when Year_SI = 2007 and
 BS_Category_VC in ('Rev','Cos','Otc','Oic','Tax') and
 Segment_VC = 'BU2' then Amount_NU else 0 end),
 sum(case when Year_SI = 2007 and
 BS_Category_VC in ('Rev','Cos','Otc','Oic','Tax') and
 Segment_VC = 'BU3' then Amount_NU else 0 end),

 sum(case when Year_SI = 2007 and
 BS_Category_VC in ('Rev','Cos','Otc','Oic','Tax')
 then Amount_NU else 0 end)as [Year to Date]

from Journal_T join COA_T
on Journal_T.GL_ID = COA_T.GL_ID
```

Now, Test your query, by clicking on the parse query button to check for any syntax error, if your syntax is working, you would see the message "The command(s) completed successfully." If not, go through the code above again, and run the parse query until your syntax is working properly. Then, execute the query, by clicking on the execute query button, you would see the following on your result pane below.

	Acct Code	Revenue	BU1	BU2	BU3	Year to Date
1	5001	Revenue_Hardware	-4000	0	0	-4000
2	5002	Revenue_Software	0	-2500	0	-2500
3	0	Total Revenue	-4000	-2500	0	-6500

	Acct Code	Cost of Sales	BU1	BU2	BU3	Year to Date
1	6001	Cost_Hardware	300	0	0	300
2	6002	Cost_Software	0	100	0	100
3	0	Total Cost of Sales	300	100	0	400
4	0	Gross Profit	-3700	-2400	0	-6100

	Acct Code	Less Other Cost	BU1	BU2	BU3	Year to Date
1	7001	Admin & Utility	0	0	1200	1200
2	7002	Prov-Stk	150	0	0	150
3	0	Total Other Cost	150	0	1200	1350

	Acct Code	Add Other Income	BU1	BU2	BU3	Year to Date
1	8001	Interest from Bank	0	-250	0	-250
2	0	Total Other Income	0	-250	0	-250
3	0	Total Operating Cost/Income	150	-250	1200	1100
4	0	Profit Before Tax (PBT)	-3550	-2650	1200	-5000
5	9001	Tax	600	0	0	600
6	0	Profit After Tax (PAT)	-2950	-2650	1200	-4400

MaxCorp, would now, be able to assess its trading performance more accurately, with the income statement created in the above format. The report tells us, that a big portion of its earnings is coming from its first business unit.

How it Works – Select Query for Income Statement by Segment

Let us continue understanding the function of the select query we have created for the above report, by looking at our first block of code.

```
select Journal_T.GL_ID as [Acct Code], GL_Name_VC as [Revenue],
 sum(case when Year_SI = 2007 and BS_Category_VC = 'Rev' and
 Segment_VC = 'BU1' then Amount_NU else 0 end) as [BU1],
 sum(case when Year_SI = 2007 and BS_Category_VC = 'Rev' and
 Segment_VC = 'BU2' then Amount_NU else 0 end) as [BU2],
 sum(case when Year_SI = 2007 and BS_Category_VC = 'Rev' and
 Segment_VC = 'BU3' then Amount_NU else 0 end) as [BU3],
 sum(case when Year_SI = 2007 then Amount_NU else 0 end)
 as [Year to Date]

from Journal_T join COA_T
on Journal_T.GL_ID = COA_T.GL_ID
where BS_Category_VC = 'Rev'
```

```
group by GL_Name_VC,Journal_T.GL_ID
```

Notice that, the above code, is similar to the set of select query, we have just created for the income statement, except, that we include an additional filtering condition, the segment name, located in the Segment_VC field. By including this piece of code, our select query, would select the appropriate records, by matching one more condition, that is, it must also contain the segment name, BU1, BU2 or BU3. By now, we should know, that, only those income or expense type, are being assigned a segment name, excluding those under the balance sheet type.

The remaining select query would work similarly as the first block of query we have discussed above, substituting the 'Rev' Category name with the remaining category we have inserted in the COA Table, and for each block, adding the additional condition for the segment type.

Besides having the above segmental report for its three business units, Dave, would also want to know, the profit level of all three business unit, by period. In order, to achieve this, we need to filter the following four field names, Period_TI, Year_SI, BS_Category_VC and Segment_VC.

Enter the following select query now

```
select Journal_T.GL_ID as [Acct Code], GL_Name_VC as [Revenue],
 sum(case when Period_TI = 8 and Year_SI = 2007 and
 BS_Category_VC = 'Rev' and Segment_VC = 'BU1' then
 Amount_NU else 0 end) as [BU1],
 sum(case when Period_TI = 8 and Year_SI = 2007 and
 BS_Category_VC = 'Rev' and Segment_VC = 'BU2' then
 Amount_NU else 0 end) as [BU2],
 sum(case when Period_TI = 8 and Year_SI = 2007 and
 BS_Category_VC = 'Rev' and Segment_VC = 'BU3' then
 Amount_NU else 0 end) as [BU3],

 sum(case when Period_TI = 8 and Year_SI = 2007 then
 Amount_NU else 0  end) as [Period 08]

from Journal_T join COA_T
on Journal_T.GL_ID = COA_T.GL_ID
where BS_Category_VC = 'Rev'
group by GL_Name_VC,Journal_T.GL_ID

union all

select 0 ,'Total Revenue',
 sum(case when Period_TI = 8 and Year_SI = 2007 and
 BS_Category_VC = 'Rev' and Segment_VC = 'BU1' then
 Amount_NU else 0 end) as [BU1],
 sum(case when Period_TI = 8 and Year_SI = 2007 and
 BS_Category_VC = 'Rev' and Segment_VC = 'BU2' then
 Amount_NU else 0 end) as [BU2],
```

```sql
 sum(case when Period_TI = 8 and Year_SI = 2007 and
 BS_Category_VC = 'Rev' and Segment_VC = 'BU3' then
 Amount_NU else 0 end) as [BU3],
 sum(case when Period_TI = 8 and Year_SI = 2007 then
 Amount_NU else 0 end) as [Period 08]

from Journal_T join COA_T
on Journal_T.GL_ID = COA_T.GL_ID
where BS_Category_VC = 'Rev'

select  Journal_T.GL_ID as  [Acct  Code],  GL_Name_VC  as  [Cost  of
Sales],
 sum(case when Period_TI = 8 and Year_SI = 2007 and
 BS_Category_VC = 'Cos' and Segment_VC = 'BU1' then
 Amount_NU else 0 end) as [BU1],
 sum(case when Period_TI = 8 and Year_SI = 2007 and
 BS_Category_VC = 'Cos' and Segment_VC = 'BU2' then
 Amount_NU else 0 end) as [BU2],
 sum(case when Period_TI = 8 and Year_SI = 2007 and
 BS_Category_VC = 'Cos' and Segment_VC = 'BU3' then
 Amount_NU else 0 end) as [BU3],
 sum(case when Period_TI = 8 and Year_SI = 2007 then
 Amount_NU else 0 end) as [Period 08]

from Journal_T join COA_T
on Journal_T.GL_ID = COA_T.GL_ID
where BS_Category_VC = 'Cos'
group by GL_Name_VC,Journal_T.GL_ID

union all

select 0 ,'Total Cost of Sales',
 sum(case when Period_TI = 8 and Year_SI = 2007 and
 BS_Category_VC = 'Cos' and Segment_VC = 'BU1' then
 Amount_NU else 0 end) as [BU1],
 sum(case when Period_TI = 8 and Year_SI = 2007 and
 BS_Category_VC = 'Cos' and Segment_VC = 'BU2' then
 Amount_NU else 0 end) as [BU2],

 sum(case when Period_TI = 8 and Year_SI = 2007 and
 BS_Category_VC = 'Cos' and Segment_VC = 'BU3' then
 Amount_NU else 0 end) as [BU3],
 sum(case when Period_TI = 8 and Year_SI = 2007 then
 Amount_NU else 0 end) as [Period 08]

from Journal_T join COA_T
on Journal_T.GL_ID = COA_T.GL_ID
where BS_Category_VC = 'Cos'

union all

select 0,'Gross Profit',
```

```sql
sum(case when Year_SI = 2007 and Period_TI = 8 and
BS_Category_VC = 'Rev' and Segment_VC = 'BU1' then
Amount_NU else 0 end)+
sum(case when Year_SI = 2007 and Period_TI = 8 and
BS_Category_VC = 'Cos' and Segment_VC = 'BU1' then
Amount_NU else 0 end)as [BU1],
sum(case when Year_SI = 2007 and Period_TI = 8 and
BS_Category_VC = 'Rev' and Segment_VC = 'BU2' then
Amount_NU else 0 end)+
sum(case when Year_SI = 2007 and Period_TI = 8 and
BS_Category_VC = 'Cos' and Segment_VC = 'BU2' then
Amount_NU else 0 end)as [BU2],
sum(case when Year_SI = 2007 and Period_TI = 8 and
BS_Category_VC = 'Rev' and Segment_VC = 'BU3' then
Amount_NU else 0 end)+
sum(case when Year_SI = 2007 and Period_TI = 8 and
BS_Category_VC = 'Cos' and Segment_VC = 'BU3' then
Amount_NU else 0 end)as [BU3],
sum(case when Year_SI = 2007 and Period_TI = 8 then
Amount_NU else 0 end)as [Period 08]

from Journal_T join COA_T
on Journal_T.GL_ID = COA_T.GL_ID
where BS_Category_VC = 'Rev'or BS_Category_VC = 'Cos'

select  Journal_T.GL_ID as [Acct Code], GL_Name_VC as [Less Other
Cost],
sum(case when Period_TI = 8 and Year_SI = 2007 and
BS_Category_VC = 'Otc' and Segment_VC = 'BU1' then
Amount_NU else 0 end) as [BU1],
sum(case when Period_TI = 8 and Year_SI = 2007 and
BS_Category_VC = 'Otc' and Segment_VC = 'BU2' then
Amount_NU else 0 end) as [BU2],
sum(case when Period_TI = 8 and Year_SI = 2007 and
BS_Category_VC = 'Otc' and Segment_VC = 'BU3' then
Amount_NU else 0 end) as [BU3],
sum(case when Period_TI = 8 and Year_SI = 2007 then
Amount_NU else 0 end) as [Period 08]

from Journal_T join COA_T
on Journal_T.GL_ID = COA_T.GL_ID
where BS_Category_VC = 'Otc'
group by GL_Name_VC,Journal_T.GL_ID

union all

select 0 ,'Total Other Cost',
sum(case when Period_TI = 8 and Year_SI = 2007 and
BS_Category_VC = 'Otc' and Segment_VC = 'BU1' then
Amount_NU else 0 end) as [BU1],
sum(case when Period_TI = 8 and Year_SI = 2007 and
BS_Category_VC = 'Otc' and Segment_VC = 'BU2' then
```

```
  Amount_NU else 0 end) as [BU2],
  sum(case when Period_TI = 8 and Year_SI = 2007 and
  BS_Category_VC = 'Otc' and Segment_VC = 'BU3' then
  Amount_NU else 0 end) as [BU3],
  sum(case when Period_TI = 8 and Year_SI = 2007 then
  Amount_NU else 0 end) as [Period 08]

from Journal_T join COA_T
on Journal_T.GL_ID = COA_T.GL_ID
where BS_Category_VC = 'Otc'

select Journal_T.GL_ID as [Acct Code],
  GL_Name_VC as [Add Other Income],
  sum(case when Period_TI = 8 and Year_SI = 2007 and
  BS_Category_VC = 'Oic' and Segment_VC = 'BU1' then
  Amount_NU else 0 end) as [BU1],
  sum(case when Period_TI = 8 and Year_SI = 2007 and
  BS_Category_VC = 'Oic' and Segment_VC = 'BU2' then
  Amount_NU else 0 end) as [BU2],
  sum(case when Period_TI = 8 and Year_SI = 2007 and
  BS_Category_VC = 'Oic' and Segment_VC = 'BU3' then
  Amount_NU else 0 end) as [BU3],
  sum(case when Period_TI = 8 and Year_SI = 2007 then
  Amount_NU else 0 end) as [Period 08]

from Journal_T join COA_T
on Journal_T.GL_ID = COA_T.GL_ID
where BS_Category_VC = 'Oic'
group by GL_Name_VC,Journal_T.GL_ID

union all

select 0 ,'Total Other Income',
  sum(case when Period_TI = 8 and Year_SI = 2007 and
  BS_Category_VC = 'Oic' and Segment_VC = 'BU1' then
  Amount_NU else 0 end) as [BU1],
  sum(case when Period_TI = 8 and Year_SI = 2007 and
  BS_Category_VC = 'Oic' and Segment_VC = 'BU2' then
  Amount_NU else 0 end) as [BU2],
  sum(case when Period_TI = 8 and Year_SI = 2007 and
  BS_Category_VC = 'Oic' and Segment_VC = 'BU3' then
  Amount_NU else 0 end) as [BU3],
  sum(case when Period_TI = 8 and Year_SI = 2007 then
  Amount_NU else 0 end) as [Period 08]

from Journal_T join COA_T
on Journal_T.GL_ID = COA_T.GL_ID
where BS_Category_VC = 'Oic'

union all

select 0,'Total Operating Cost/Income',
```

```sql
sum(case when Year_SI = 2007 and Period_TI = 8 and
BS_Category_VC = 'Otc' and Segment_VC = 'BU1' then
Amount_NU else 0 end)+
sum(case when Year_SI = 2007 and Period_TI = 8 and
BS_Category_VC = 'Oic' and Segment_VC = 'BU1' then
Amount_NU else 0 end)as [BU1],
sum(case when Year_SI = 2007 and Period_TI = 8 and
BS_Category_VC = 'Otc' and Segment_VC = 'BU2' then
Amount_NU else 0 end)+
sum(case when Year_SI = 2007 and Period_TI = 8 and
BS_Category_VC = 'Oic' and Segment_VC = 'BU2' then
Amount_NU else 0 end)as [BU2],
sum(case when Year_SI = 2007 and Period_TI = 8 and
BS_Category_VC = 'Otc' and Segment_VC = 'BU3' then
Amount_NU else 0 end)+
sum(case when Year_SI = 2007 and Period_TI = 8 and
BS_Category_VC = 'Oic' and Segment_VC = 'BU3' then
Amount_NU else 0 end)as [BU3],
sum(case when Year_SI = 2007 and Period_TI = 8 then
Amount_NU else 0 end)as [Period 08]

from Journal_T join COA_T
on Journal_T.GL_ID = COA_T.GL_ID
where BS_Category_VC = 'Otc'or BS_Category_VC = 'Oic'

union all

select 0, 'Profit Before Tax (PBT)',
 sum(case when Period_TI = 8 and Year_SI = 2007 and
 BS_Category_VC in ('Rev','Cos','Otc','Oic') and
 Segment_VC = 'BU1' then Amount_NU else 0 end),
 sum(case when Period_TI = 8 and Year_SI = 2007 and
 BS_Category_VC in ('Rev','Cos','Otc','Oic') and
 Segment_VC = 'BU2' then Amount_NU else 0 end),
 sum(case when Period_TI = 8 and Year_SI = 2007 and
 BS_Category_VC in ('Rev','Cos','Otc','Oic') and
 Segment_VC = 'BU3' then Amount_NU else 0 end),
 sum(case when Year_SI = 2007 and Period_TI = 8 then
 Amount_NU else 0 end)as [Period 08]

from Journal_T join COA_T
on Journal_T.GL_ID = COA_T.GL_ID
where BS_Category_VC in ('Rev','Cos','Otc','Oic')

select Journal_T.GL_ID as [Acct Code], GL_Name_VC as [Income Tax],
 sum(case when Period_TI = 8 and Year_SI = 2007 and
 BS_Category_VC = 'Tax' and Segment_VC = 'BU1' then
 Amount_NU else 0 end) as [BU1],
 sum(case when Period_TI = 8 and Year_SI = 2007 and
 BS_Category_VC = 'Tax' and Segment_VC = 'BU2' then
 Amount_NU else 0 end) as [BU2],
 sum(case when Period_TI = 8 and Year_SI = 2007 and
```

```
BS_Category_VC = 'Tax' and Segment_VC = 'BU3' then
Amount_NU else 0 end) as [BU3],
sum(case when Period_TI = 8 and Year_SI = 2007 then
Amount_NU else 0 end) as [Period 08]

from Journal_T join COA_T
on Journal_T.GL_ID = COA_T.GL_ID
where BS_Category_VC = 'Tax'
group by GL_Name_VC,Journal_T.GL_ID

union all

select 0, 'Profit After Tax (PAT)',
sum(case when Period_TI = 8 and Year_SI = 2007 and
BS_Category_VC in ('Rev','Cos','Otc','Oic','Tax') and
Segment_VC = 'BU1' then Amount_NU else 0 end),
sum(case when Period_TI = 8 and Year_SI = 2007 and
BS_Category_VC in ('Rev','Cos','Otc','Oic','Tax') and
Segment_VC = 'BU2' then Amount_NU else 0 end),
sum(case when Period_TI = 8 and Year_SI = 2007 and
BS_Category_VC in ('Rev','Cos','Otc','Oic','Tax') and
Segment_VC = 'BU3' then Amount_NU else 0 end),
sum(case when Period_TI = 8 and Year_SI = 2007 and
BS_Category_VC in ('Rev','Cos','Otc','Oic','Tax') then
Amount_NU else 0 end)as [Month to Date]

from Journal_T join COA_T
on Journal_T.GL_ID = COA_T.GL_ID
```

Now, Test your query, by clicking on the parse query button to check for any syntax error, if your syntax is working, you would see the message "The command(s) completed successfully." If not, go through the code above again, and run the parse query until your syntax is working properly. Then, execute the query, by clicking on the execute query button, you would see the following on your result pane below.

	Acct Code	Revenue	BU1	BU2	BU3	Period 08
1	5001	Revenue_Hardware	-2000	0	0	-2000
2	5002	Revenue_Software	0	0	0	0
3	0	Total Revenue	-2000	0	0	-2000

	Acct Code	Cost of Sales	BU1	BU2	BU3	Period 08
1	6001	Cost_Hardware	150	0	0	150
2	6002	Cost_Software	0	0	0	0
3	0	Total Cost of Sales	150	0	0	150
4	0	Gross Profit	-1850	0	0	-1850

	Acct Code	Less Other Cost	BU1	BU2	BU3	Period 08
1	7001	Admin & Utility	0	0	0	0
2	7002	Prov-Stk	0	0	0	0
3	0	Total Other Cost	0	0	0	0

	Acct Code	Add Other Income	BU1	BU2	BU3	Period 08
1	8001	Interest from Bank	0	0	0	0
2	0	Total Other Income	0	0	0	0
3	0	Total Operating Cost/Income	0	0	0	0
4	0	Profit Before Tax (PBT)	-1850	0	0	-1850

	Acct Code	Income Tax	BU1	BU2	BU3	Period 08
1	9001	Tax	0	0	0	0
2	0	Profit After Tax (PAT)	-1850	0	0	-1850

Grids Messages

The above result shows us the trading performance of MaxCorp, by business unit, in Period 8, in the month of August, 2007. We know at this stage, that, in order to produce such report, we only include the additional filtering condition for the period.

4) Using SQL to produce Balance Sheet

This report would generally produce the asset, liability, accumulating profit and capital of MaxCorp as of to date, at their carrying amount. This balance sheet elements, are continuous in nature, in that, their amount are carried forward continuously, year after year, unlike profit or loss element which accumulates up to a full year only, before it finally adds up to the accumulated profits account, appearing as a balance sheet item in the balance sheet statement, at the close of each financial year.

Let us enter the following select query for creating the balance sheet report, now :

```
select 'Cur_yr_Earnings' as [Share Capital & Earnings],
 sum(case when COA_T.BS_Category_VC in
 ('Rev','Cos','Otc','Oic','Tax')
 and Journal_T.Year_SI = 2007
 then Journal_T.Amount_NU else 0 end) as [$]

from COA_T join Journal_T
on COA_T.GL_ID = Journal_T.GL_ID

union all

select GL_Name_VC,
 sum(case when Year_SI = 2007 and BS_Category_VC in ('SF') then
 Amount_NU else 0 end) as [$]

from COA_T join Journal_T
on COA_T.GL_ID = Journal_T.GL_ID
where Year_SI = 2007
and BS_Category_VC in ('SF')
group by GL_Name_VC

union all

select 'Total Shareholder Funds' as [Liabilities and Capital],
 sum(case when BS_Category_VC in ('Rev','Cos','Otc','Oic','Tax') and
 Year_SI = 2007
 then Amount_NU else 0 end) +
 sum(case when Year_SI = 2007 and BS_Category_VC in ('SF') then
 Amount_NU else 0 end) as [$]

from COA_T join Journal_T
on COA_T.GL_ID = Journal_T.GL_ID

select   isnull(GL_Name_VC,  'Total   Current   Liability')as   [Current
Liabilities], sum(Amount_NU)as [$]

from COA_T join Journal_T
on COA_T.GL_ID = Journal_T.GL_ID
where BS_Category_VC = 'CL'
group by GL_Name_VC
with rollup

select  SUM(case when BS_Category_VC ='CL' or BS_Category_VC='SF'
 then Amount_NU else 0 end) +
 sum(case when BS_Category_VC in ('Rev','Cos','Otc','Oic','Tax') and
 Year_SI = 2007
```

```
  then Amount_NU else 0 end) AS [Total Liabilities]

from COA_T join Journal_T
on COA_T.GL_ID = Journal_T.GL_ID

select isnull(GL_Name_VC, 'Total Net Book Value')as [Fixed Assets],
 sum(Amount_NU)as [$]

from COA_T join Journal_T
on COA_T.GL_ID = Journal_T.GL_ID
where BS_Category_VC in ('FA','FA_Cost')
group by GL_Name_VC
with rollup

select isnull(GL_Name_VC, 'Total Current Asset')as [Current Asset],
 sum(Amount_NU)as [$]

from COA_T join Journal_T
on COA_T.GL_ID = Journal_T.GL_ID
where BS_Category_VC='CA'
group by GL_Name_VC
with rollup

select  SUM(Amount_NU)AS [Total Assets]

from COA_T join Journal_T
on COA_T.GL_ID = Journal_T.GL_ID
where BS_Category_VC='CA' or BS_Category_VC in ('FA','FA_Cost')
```

Now, Test your query, by clicking on the parse query button to check for any syntax error, if your syntax is working, you would see the message "The command(s) completed successfully." If not, go through the code above again, and run the parse query until your syntax is working properly. Then, execute the query, by clicking on the execute query button, and you would see the following output appearing on your result pane

	Share Capital & Earnings	$
1	Cur_yr_Earnings	-4400
2	RE b/f	965
3	Share_Cap	-2000
4	Total Shareholder Funds	-5435

	Current Liabilities	$
1	Creditors	-2310
2	Total Current Liabil	-2310

	Total Liabilities	
1	-7745	

	Fixed Assets	$
1	Acc_Deprn	-1000
2	PPE	2900
3	Total Net Book Value	1900

	Current Asset	$
1	Bank	3195
2	Debtor	2500
3	Prov_ Stk_Obsolete	-150
4	Stock	300
5	Total Current Asset	5845

	Total Assets	
1	7745	

Notice, that, the Total Assets has similar amount as in the Total Liabilities, this shows that, all the accounts balance, as summing up the total assets and liabilities would yield a 0 amount.

How it Works – Select Query for Balance Sheet

Let us analyze the function of our first block of select query:

```
select 'Cur_yr_Earnings' as [Share Capital & Earnings],
 sum(case when COA_T.BS_Category_VC in
 ('Rev','Cos','Otc','Oic','Tax')
 and Journal_T.Year_SI = 2007
 then Journal_T.Amount_NU else 0 end) as [$]

from COA_T join Journal_T
on COA_T.GL_ID = Journal_T.GL_ID
```

Our first selection, does not select any field, merely indicating the word 'Cur_yr_Earnings', to appear on the first column. We know that, the current year earnings amount of $4,400, is the profit generated in Year 2007, thus we sum up all the income and expense elements, to derive the profit after tax, to be our second column.

Next, we join the second block using the union all clause.

```
union all

select GL_Name_VC,
 sum(case when Year_SI = 2007 and BS_Category_VC in ('SF') then
 Amount_NU else 0 end) as [$]

from COA_T join Journal_T
on COA_T.GL_ID = Journal_T.GL_ID
where Year_SI = 2007
and BS_Category_VC in ('SF')
group by GL_Name_VC
```

Our first column, will select the account name that are categorized as 'SF' category, in the Year 2007, next we sum up its corresponding amount to appear on the second column. Again, we join our third block of code,

```
union all

select 'Total Shareholder Funds' as [Liabilities and Capital],
 sum(case when BS_Category_VC in ('Rev','Cos','Otc','Oic','Tax') and
 Year_SI = 2007
 then Amount_NU else 0 end) +
 sum(case when Year_SI = 2007 and BS_Category_VC in ('SF') then
 Amount_NU else 0 end) as [$]

from COA_T join Journal_T
on COA_T.GL_ID = Journal_T.GL_ID
```

We create a subtotal, called "Total Shareholder Funds", on the first column, and sum up the amount for the first and second block to appear as a summation, on the second column.

The following block of the above select query, would perform the same function, by just, substituting the BS_Category_VC's category name with the rest of the category name, specifying the Year to be '2007'.

5) Using SQL to produce Transaction Listing

This would generally shows the movement of each account code in a particular range of period. This means, Dave would want to see the debit and credit entries being recorded for each account code, captured in the Journal Table. We will first, create the first block of select query for a balance sheet type, account code, and then for the income and expense type account code, in our second block of query.

Let us start, by entering the following select query for extracting the debit and credit entries for a balance sheet type account code,

```
select '' as [Date],'' as [Acct Code], 'Opening Balance' as
 [Acct   Name],Descrip_VC  as  [Description],0  as  [Period  Dr],0  as
[Period Cr],0 as [Net Change],sum(Amount_NU)as [Closing Bal]

from COA_T join Journal_T
on COA_T.GL_ID = Journal_T.GL_ID
where Year_SI < 2007
and BS_Category_VC in ('CA')
and Journal_T.GL_ID = 2003
group by Descrip_VC

union all

select
 convert(varchar,Date_DT,3),Journal_T.GL_ID,GL_Name_VC,Descrip_VC,
 [Period Dr] = sum( case when Amount_NU >0 and Year_SI = 2007 then
 Amount_NU else 0 end),
 [Period Cr] = sum( case when Amount_NU <0 and Year_SI = 2007 then
 Amount_NU else 0 end),
 sum(Amount_NU)as [Net Change],[Closing Bal] = sum(Amount_NU)

from Journal_T join COA_T
on Journal_T.GL_ID = COA_T.GL_ID
where Year_SI = 2007 and Journal_T.GL_ID = 2003
group by Journal_T.GL_ID,Date_DT,GL_Name_VC,Descrip_VC

union all

select '','', 'Total Balance','',
sum(case when Year_SI = 2007 and Amount_NU > 0 then Amount_NU else 0
end),
sum(case when Year_SI = 2007 and Amount_NU < 0 then Amount_NU else 0
end),
sum(case  when  Year_SI  =  2007  then  Amount_NU  else  0  end),
sum(Amount_NU)

from Journal_T join COA_T
on Journal_T.GL_ID = COA_T.GL_ID
```

```
where Year_SI = 2007 and Journal_T.GL_ID = 2003 OR Year_SI < 2007
and Journal_T.GL_ID = 2003 and BS_Category_VC in ('CA')
```

Now, Test your query, by clicking on the parse query button to check for any syntax error, if your syntax is working, you would see the message "The command(s) completed successfully." If not, go through the code above again, and run the parse query until your syntax is working properly. Then, execute the query, by clicking on the execute query button, and you would see the following output appearing on your result pane.

	Date	Acct Code	Acct Name	Description	Period Dr	Period Cr	Net Change	Closing Bal
1	12/05/07	2003	Debtor	HP Presario-TX 101 P4	2000	0	2000	2000
2	22/08/07	2003	Debtor	HP Presario-TX 101 P4	2000	0	2000	2000
3	23/07/07	2003	Debtor	Receipt frm Randy	0	-2000	-2000	-2000
4	26/08/07	2003	Debtor	Receipt frm William	0	-2000	-2000	-2000
5	03/06/07	2003	Debtor	Red Hat-version 2.0	2500	0	2500	2500
6		0	Total Balance		6500	-4000	2500	2500

How it Works – Select Query for Transaction Listing

Notice, our select query, has created eight columns. Let us look at our first block of code,

```
select '' as [Date],'' as [Acct Code], 'Opening Balance' as
 [Acct  Name],Descrip_VC  as  [Description],0  as  [Period  Dr],0  as
[Period Cr],0 as [Net Change],sum(Amount_NU)as [Closing Bal]

from COA_T join Journal_T
on COA_T.GL_ID = Journal_T.GL_ID
where Year_SI < 2007
and BS_Category_VC in ('CA')
and Journal_T.GL_ID = 2003
group by Descrip_VC
```

We know that, a balance sheet type element would carry its amount continuously, year after year. We want to sum up the entire amount for a particular account code, in this case, the Debtor code, 2003, that was recorded in the Journal Table, before Year 2007, and to place the summation on the eighth column, giving the description, "Opening Balance". We do not want to capture records, captured before Year 2007; thus, we quote the 0 figure to appear on the 5th, 6th and 7th column. As you may know, we do not have any entry that was captured before Year 2007 for the account code 2003, in our Journal Table; therefore, we would not see an Opening Balance on the Transaction Listing above. However, we can test whether our code is working, by changing one of the Debtors record's year to a previous year, and then try running the query again. This time, you might see an Opening Balance.

Our next block of code, follows ;

```
union all

select
 convert(varchar,Date_DT,3),Journal_T.GL_ID,GL_Name_VC,Descrip_VC,
 [Period Dr] = sum( case when Amount_NU >0 and Year_SI = 2007 then
 Amount_NU else 0 end),
 [Period Cr] = sum( case when Amount_NU <0 and Year_SI = 2007 then
 Amount_NU else 0 end),
 sum(Amount_NU)as [Net Change],
 [Closing Bal] = sum(Amount_NU)

from Journal_T join COA_T
on Journal_T.GL_ID = COA_T.GL_ID
where Year_SI = 2007 and Journal_T.GL_ID = 2003
group by Journal_T.GL_ID,Date_DT,GL_Name_VC,Descrip_VC
```

First, we select the date, applying the conversion function, to format our date in the preferred format as dd/mm/yyyy. Next, we select the account code, 2003, its account name, and description and place them on their respective column, we then sum up those amount which are greater than 0 as Debit amount, and those lesser than 0, as credit amount. We sum up both the debit and credit, and place it as a summation on the Net Change column, and we create a closing balance column to add both debit and credit amount.

```
union all

select '','', 'Total Balance','',
sum(case when Year_SI = 2007 and Amount_NU > 0 then Amount_NU else 0
end),
sum(case when Year_SI = 2007 and Amount_NU < 0 then Amount_NU else 0
end),
sum(case when Year_SI = 2007 then Amount_NU else 0 end),
sum(Amount_NU)

from Journal_T join COA_T
on Journal_T.GL_ID = COA_T.GL_ID
where Year_SI = 2007 and Journal_T.GL_ID = 2003 OR Year_SI < 2007
and Journal_T.GL_ID = 2003 and BS_Category_VC in ('CA')
```

We then join our next block of code, as a total balance of all the individual columns, of which, we have created in our previous block, adding all debit and credit amount, captured in all the years.

Next, we enter the following select query for extracting the debit and credit entries for an income type account code,

```
select '' as [Date],'' as [Acct Code], 'Opening Balance' as [Acct
```

```
 Name],Descrip_VC as  [Description],0 as  [Period Dr],0 as  [Period
Cr],0 as [Net Change],sum(Amount_NU)as [Closing Bal]

from Journal_T join COA_T
on Journal_T.GL_ID = COA_T.GL_ID
where Year_SI = 2007
and BS_Category_VC in ('Rev')
and Period_TI = 1
and Journal_T.GL_ID IN (5001,5002)
group by Descrip_VC

union all

select
 convert(varchar,Date_DT,3),Journal_T.GL_ID,GL_Name_VC,Descrip_VC,
 [Period Dr] = sum( case when Amount_NU >0 and Year_SI = 2007 and
 Period_TI > 1 then Amount_NU else 0 end),
 [Period Cr] = sum( case when Amount_NU <0 and Year_SI = 2007 and
 Period_TI > 1 then Amount_NU else 0 end),
 sum(Amount_NU)as [Net Change],
 [Closing Bal] = sum(Amount_NU)

from Journal_T join COA_T
on Journal_T.GL_ID = COA_T.GL_ID
where Year_SI = 2007 and Journal_T.GL_ID in (5001,5002)and
Period_TI > 1
group by Journal_T.GL_ID,Date_DT,GL_Name_VC,Descrip_VC

union all

select '','', 'Total Balance','',
 sum(case when Year_SI = 2007 and Amount_NU > 0 and Period_TI > 1
then
 Amount_NU else 0 end),
 sum(case when Year_SI = 2007 and Amount_NU < 0 and Period_TI > 1
then
 Amount_NU else 0 end),
 sum(case when Year_SI = 2007 and Period_TI > 1 then Amount_NU else
0 end),sum(Amount_NU)

from Journal_T join COA_T
on Journal_T.GL_ID = COA_T.GL_ID
where Year_SI = 2007 and Journal_T.GL_ID in (5001,5002)
```

Now, Test your query, by clicking on the parse query button to check for any syntax error, if your syntax is working, you would see the message "The command(s) completed successfully." If not, go through the code above again, and run the parse query until your syntax is working properly. Then, execute the query, by clicking on the execute query button, and you would see the following output appearing on your result pane.

	Date	Acct Code	Acct Name	Description	Period Dr	Period Cr	Net Change	Closing Bal
1	12/05/07	5001	Revenue_Hardware	HP Presario-TX 101 P4	0	-2000	-2000	-2000
2	22/08/07	5001	Revenue_Hardware	HP Presario-TX 101 P4	0	-2000	-2000	-2000
3	03/06/07	5002	Revenue_Software	Red Hat-version 2.0	0	-2500	-2500	-2500
4		0	Total Balance		0	-6500	-6500	-6500

Notice, that the above transaction listing is not much different from the previous transaction listing, we have created just now. Let us go through our first block of code,

```
select '' as [Date],'' as [Acct Code], 'Opening Balance' as [Acct
 Name],Descrip_VC as [Description],0 as [Period Dr],0 as [Period
Cr],0 as [Net Change],sum(Amount_NU)as [Closing Bal]

from Journal_T join COA_T
on Journal_T.GL_ID = COA_T.GL_ID
where Year_SI = 2007
and BS_Category_VC in ('Rev')
and Period_TI = 1
and Journal_T.GL_ID IN (5001,5002)
group by Descrip_VC
```

Unlike a balance sheet element, an income or expense element does not carries its amount continuously year after year, it would only carry its amount within a year, and will eventually adds up to the accumulated profits after ending period 12, appearing as a balance sheet element in the balance sheet. As in our above case, we would only see an Opening Balance in the Revenue account code (5001 and 5002), if there exist entries that fall on period 1, in Year 2007, as we have indicated under the query "and Period_TI = 1"

In the subsequent select query, we would extract those revenue (5001 and 5002) account's entries that are captured after period 01 in Year 2007, and place them in their respective columns as shown on our next block of query.

```
union all

select
 convert(varchar,Date_DT,3),Journal_T.GL_ID,GL_Name_VC,Descrip_VC,
 [Period Dr] = sum( case when Amount_NU >0 and Year_SI = 2007 and
 Period_TI > 1 then Amount_NU else 0 end),
 [Period Cr] = sum( case when Amount_NU <0 and Year_SI = 2007 and
 Period_TI > 1 then Amount_NU else 0 end),
 sum(Amount_NU)as [Net Change],
 [Closing Bal] = sum(Amount_NU)

from Journal_T join COA_T
on Journal_T.GL_ID = COA_T.GL_ID
where Year_SI = 2007 and Journal_T.GL_ID in (5001,5002)and
Period_TI > 1
```

```
group by Journal_T.GL_ID,Date_DT,GL_Name_VC,Descrip_VC
```

We then, add up all the individual columns, and place them as a summation under the Total Balance row.

```
union all

select '','', 'Total Balance','',
 sum(case when Year_SI = 2007 and Amount_NU > 0 and Period_TI > 1
then
 Amount_NU else 0 end),
 sum(case when Year_SI = 2007 and Amount_NU < 0 and Period_TI > 1
then
 Amount_NU else 0 end),
 sum(case when Year_SI = 2007 and Period_TI > 1 then Amount_NU else
0 end),sum(Amount_NU)

from Journal_T join COA_T
on Journal_T.GL_ID = COA_T.GL_ID
where Year_SI = 2007 and Journal_T.GL_ID in (5001,5002)
```

Summary

In Chapter 8, we learned how to create reports from the Journal Table, applying the Transact-SQL to perform the select query to produce the necessary accounting reports required by MaxCorp.

To summarize, in this chapter, we have discussed:

- How to create select query to produce a trial balance

- How to create select query to produce an income statement

- How to create select query to produce an income statement by segment

- How to create select query to produce an income statement by period

- How to create select query to produce a balance sheet

- How to create select query to produce a transaction listing (balance sheet item)

- How to create select query to produce a transaction listing (income/expense item)

Chapter 9

Creating Reports from Inventory Table

We have just completed Chapter 8, discussing, how to create reports from the Journal Table, now, it is time to generate some reports from the Inventory Table for Dave. Dave has mentioned that he would like to have the following list of reports for MaxCorp's inventory.

1) Stock Movement Report
2) Stock Ageing & Balance Report

1) Using SQL to produce Stock Movement Report

Let us begin, by entering the following test data in each of the tables:

Stock_Movement_T

Doc_No_VC	Date_DT	Pdt_ID_VC	Qty_NU	Unit_Price_TI	Descrip_VC
JV1002	6/3/2007	1235	-50	2	DO103
JV1003	7/20/2006	1234	60	5	GRN001
JV1000	5/12/2007	1234	-30	5	DO100
JV1004	7/20/2006	1234	30	6	GRN002
JV1005	7/20/2006	1235	110	2	GRN003
JV1001	8/22/2007	1234	-30	5	DO102

Save your table, once you have completed entering the above data, next enter the following select query,

```
select  convert(varchar,Date_DT,3)  as  [Transaction date], Pdt_ID_VC
as
 [Product Code],Descrip_VC as [Doc Number],Qty_NU as
 [Qty],Unit_Price_TI as [Unit Price],
 sum(case when Qty_NU > 0 then Qty_NU * Unit_Price_TI else 0 end) as
 [Debit],
 sum(case when Qty_NU < 0 then Qty_NU * Unit_Price_TI else 0 end)as
 [Credit]

from Stock_Movement_T
group by Date_DT,Pdt_ID_VC,Descrip_VC,Qty_NU,Unit_Price_TI

union all

select '','','Balance Qty: ' + Pdt_ID_VC,
 sum(Qty_NU),0,0,0
```

```
from Stock_Movement_T
where Pdt_ID_VC = 1234
group by Pdt_ID_VC

union all

select '','','Balance Qty: ' + Pdt_ID_VC,
 sum(Qty_NU),0,0,0

from Stock_Movement_T
where Pdt_ID_VC = 1235
group by Pdt_ID_VC

union all

select '','','Closing Stock Value for: ' + Pdt_ID_VC,
 sum(case when Qty_NU > 0 then Qty_NU * Unit_Price_TI else 0 end) +
 sum(case when Qty_NU < 0 then Qty_NU * Unit_Price_TI else 0
end),0,0,0

from Stock_Movement_T
where Pdt_ID_VC = 1234
group by Pdt_ID_VC

union all

select '','','Closing Stock Value for: ' +  Pdt_ID_VC,
 sum(case when Qty_NU > 0 then Qty_NU * Unit_Price_TI else 0 end) +
 sum(case when Qty_NU < 0 then Qty_NU * Unit_Price_TI else 0
end),0,0,0

from Stock_Movement_T
where Pdt_ID_VC = 1235
group by Pdt_ID_VC
```

Next, test your query, by clicking on the parse query button to check for any syntax error, if your syntax is working, you would see the message "The command(s) completed successfully." If not, go through the code above again, and run the parse query until your syntax is working properly. Then, execute the query, by clicking on the execute query button, and you would see the following output appearing on your result pane.

	Transaction date	Product Code	Doc Number	Qty	Unit Price	Debit	Credit
1	20/07/06	1234	GRN001	60	5	300	0
2	20/07/06	1234	GRN002	30	6	180	0
3	20/07/06	1235	GRN003	110	2	220	0
4	12/05/07	1234	DO100	-30	5	0	-150
5	03/06/07	1235	DO103	-50	2	0	-100
6	22/08/07	1234	DO102	-30	5	0	-150
7			Balance Qty: 1234	30	0	0	0
8			Balance Qty: 1235	60	0	0	0
9			Closing Stock Value for: 1234	180	0	0	0
10			Closing Stock Value for: 1235	120	0	0	0

Our Stock Movement report above has include a row for showing the balance of each product item quantity, and its remaining stock value existing in MaxCorp's warehouse.

How It Works – Select Query for Stock Movement Report

Let us run through our first block of code,

```
select  convert(varchar,Date_DT,3) as [Transaction date], Pdt_ID_VC
as [Product Code],Descrip_VC as [Doc Number],Qty_NU as [Qty],
Unit_Price_TI as [Unit Price],
 sum(case when Qty_NU > 0 then Qty_NU * Unit_Price_TI else 0 end) as
 [Debit],
 sum(case when Qty_NU < 0 then Qty_NU * Unit_Price_TI else 0 end)as
 [Credit]

from Stock_Movement_T
group by Date_DT,Pdt_ID_VC,Descrip_VC,Qty_NU,Unit_Price_TI
```

Here, we select the date to be our first item to appear on our first column, formatting it as dd/mm/yyyy. Then, we extract the product code; follow by its description, quantity, and unit price. We compute the value of each transaction, by multiplying its quantity against its unit price, and then place them on the debit column, if the amount is greater than 0, and on the credit column, if the amount is lesser than 0. We will then, sort our result, first, by date, next, by product code, description, quantity and then by unit price.

Let us look at our second block of code as follows ;

```
union all

select '','','Balance Qty: ' + Pdt_ID_VC,
 sum(Qty_NU),0,0,0

from Stock_Movement_T
```

```
where Pdt_ID_VC = 1234
group by Pdt_ID_VC
```

We sum up the quantity balance, by adding up all records residing under the Qty_NU field, for product item, 1234.

```
union all

select '','','Closing Stock Value for: ' + Pdt_ID_VC,
  sum(case when Qty_NU > 0 then Qty_NU * Unit_Price_TI else 0 end) +
  sum(case when Qty_NU < 0 then Qty_NU * Unit_Price_TI else 0
end),0,0,0

from Stock_Movement_T
where Pdt_ID_VC = 1234
group by Pdt_ID_VC
```

We then, compute each product items' stock value, by adding both amounts that are greater and lesser than 0, for product code: 1234.

We apply the same concept for product 1235, in which we have created above.

2) Using SQL to produce Stock Ageing & Balance Report

This report would, show the balance and age of each product item purchased by MaxCorp. The age of each stock will tell Dave, how long the inventory has been kept in MaxCorp warehouse.

Let us first, enter the following test data into the Stock_Balance Table as follows:

Stock_Balance_T				
Doc_ID_VC	Pdt_ID_VC	Qty_NU	Unit_Price_TI	Date_DT
RZE100	1234	30	6	8/22/2007
RST100	1235	60	2	6/3/2007

Now, let us create the select query for the Stock Ageing & Balance Report,

```
Select Pdt_ID_VC as [Product Code],convert(varchar(08),Date_DT,3) as
  [Date],Qty_NU as [Qty],convert(varchar,Unit_Price_TI) as [Unit
Price],
  (case when (getdate() - (Date_DT)) between 0 and 29.99
  then (Unit_Price_TI * Qty_NU) else 0 end) as [0 - 30 Days],
  (case when (getdate() - (Date_DT)) between 30 and 59.99
  then (Unit_Price_TI * Qty_NU) else 0 end) as [31 - 60 Days],
  (case when (getdate() - (Date_DT)) between 60 and 89.99
  then (Unit_Price_TI * Qty_NU) else 0 end) as [61 - 90 Days],
  (case when (getdate() - (Date_DT)) >= 90
```

```
then (Unit_Price_TI * Qty_NU) else 0 end) as [ > 90 Days]

from Stock_Balance_T
group by Date_DT,Pdt_ID_VC,Qty_NU,Unit_Price_TI

union all

select 0,'0',0,'Total',
 sum(case when (getdate() - (Date_DT)) between 0 and 29.99
 then (Unit_Price_TI * Qty_NU) else 0 end)as [0 - 30 Days],
 sum(case when (getdate() - (Date_DT)) between 30 and 59.99
 then (Unit_Price_TI * Qty_NU) else 0 end)as [31 - 60 Days],
 sum(case when (getdate() - (Date_DT)) between 60 and 89.99
 then (Unit_Price_TI * Qty_NU) else 0 end)as [61 - 90 Days],
 sum(case when (getdate() - (Date_DT)) >= 90
 then (Unit_Price_TI * Qty_NU) else 0 end)as [ > 90 Days]

from Stock_Balance_T
```

Now, Test your query, by clicking on the parse query button to check for any syntax error, if your syntax is working, you would see the message "The command(s) completed successfully." If not, go through the code above again, and run the parse query until your syntax is working properly. Then, execute the query, by clicking on the execute query button, and you would see the following output appearing on your result pane.

	Product Code	Date	Qty	Unit Price	0 – 30 Days	31 – 60 Days	61 – 90 Days	> 90 Days
1	1235	03/06/07	60	2	0	0	0	120
2	1234	22/08/07	30	6	0	0	0	180
3	0	0	0	Total	0	0	0	300

How It Works – Select Query for Stock Ageing & Balance Report

From the above result, we can tell that, both of the product code, has been kept in MaxCorp's warehouse for more than 90 days. The sum of these two products' value equals to the closing stock value, appearing on the balance sheet.

Let us analyze the function of our first section,

```
Select Pdt_ID_VC as [Product Code],convert(varchar(08),Date_DT,3) as
 [Date],Qty_NU   as   [Qty],convert(varchar,Unit_Price_TI)   as   [Unit
Price],
 (case when (getdate() - (Date_DT)) between 0 and 29.99
 then (Unit_Price_TI * Qty_NU) else 0 end) as [0 - 30 Days],
 (case when (getdate() - (Date_DT)) between 30 and 59.99
 then (Unit_Price_TI * Qty_NU) else 0 end) as [31 - 60 Days],
 (case when (getdate() - (Date_DT)) between 60 and 89.99
 then (Unit_Price_TI * Qty_NU) else 0 end) as [61 - 90 Days],
```

```
(case when (getdate() - (Date_DT)) >= 90
then (Unit_Price_TI * Qty_NU) else 0 end) as [ > 90 Days]

from Stock_Balance_T
group by Date_DT,Pdt_ID_VC,Qty_NU,Unit_Price_TI
```

As appears on the result pane, the first column will depict the product code, next its date of transaction, its quantity and unit price. We apply the date function, next, specifying the period range in days, in which, each of the product would fit in, slotting them in their respective range of days. It shows how long, each of the product items has been sitting in MaxCorp's warehouse, base on their last updated date.

We then, sum up the total of each column, giving a total summation, and join them together with the first block of code.

```
union all

select 0,'0',0,'Total',
 sum(case when (getdate() - (Date_DT)) between 0 and 29.99
 then (Unit_Price_TI * Qty_NU) else 0 end)as [0 - 30 Days],
 sum(case when (getdate() - (Date_DT)) between 30 and 59.99
 then (Unit_Price_TI * Qty_NU) else 0 end)as [31 - 60 Days],
 sum(case when (getdate() - (Date_DT)) between 60 and 89.99
 then (Unit_Price_TI * Qty_NU) else 0 end)as [61 - 90 Days],
 sum(case when (getdate() - (Date_DT)) >= 90
 then (Unit_Price_TI * Qty_NU) else 0 end)as [ > 90 Days]

from Stock_Balance_T
```

Summary

In Chapter 9, we have learned how to create reports from the Inventory Table, applying the Transact-SQL to perform the select query to produce the necessary accounting reports required by MaxCorp.

To summarize, in this chapter, we have discussed:

> ➢ How to create select query to produce a Stock Movement Report

> ➢ How to create select query to produce a Stock Ageing & Balance Report

Chapter 10

Creating Reports from Purchase Table

Dave wants to have a list of the following reports from the Purchase Table we have created for MaxCorp in Chapter 4.

1) Accounts Payable Ageing Report
2) Accounts Payable Payment Status Report

Let us enter some test data into the following tables listed as follows:

Purchase_T

Cred_ID_VC	Pdt_ID_VC	Doc_No_VC	Date_DT	Status_BT	Inv_ID_VC
CRE101	1234	JV1003	7/20/2006	0	IN100
CRE101	1234	JV1004	7/20/2006	0	IN101
CRE100	1235	JV1005	7/20/2006	0	IN102
CRE103		JV1010	12/28/2006	1	1256
CRE102		JV1013	2/20/2007	0	1257

Creditor_T

Cred_ID_VC	Cred_Name_VC	Cred_Add_VC	Cred_Contact_VC	Credit_Term_TI	Cred_Code_IN
CRE101	Supplier1	56th Georgia	458787	30	3000
CRE100	Supplier2	34th Alm Street	145432	45	3000
CRE103	Furniturer2	7th Roland	121212	60	3000
CRE102	Furniturer1	7th Roland	121212	45	3000

1) Using SQL to produce Accounts Payable Ageing Report

Let us enter the following select query, now

```
SELECT
 Cred_Name_VC   as   [Creditor   Name],   Inv_ID_VC   as   [Inv   No],
Credit_Term_TI as [Credit Term],Journal_T.Doc_No_VC as [Doc No],
 convert(varchar,Purchase_T.Date_DT,3) as InvoiceDate,
 DATEDIFF(day, Purchase_T.Date_DT+Credit_Term_TI, getdate()) as
 [Days Overdue],
 convert(varchar,DATEADD(day,Credit_Term_TI,Purchase_T.Date_DT),3)as
 Due_date,

 (CASE WHEN (GETDATE() - (Purchase_T.Date_DT+Credit_Term_TI))
 BETWEEN - 100 AND 29.99 THEN Journal_T.Amount_NU ELSE 0 END) AS
 Less_than_30_DYS,
 (CASE WHEN (GETDATE() - (Purchase_T.Date_DT+Credit_Term_TI))
 BETWEEN 30 AND 59.99 THEN Journal_T.Amount_NU ELSE 0 END) AS
```

```
'> 30 DYS',
(CASE WHEN (GETDATE() - (Purchase_T.Date_DT+Credit_Term_TI))
BETWEEN 60 AND 89.99 THEN Journal_T.Amount_NU ELSE 0 END) AS
'> 60 DYS',
(CASE WHEN (GETDATE() - (Purchase_T.Date_DT+Credit_Term_TI))
>= 90 THEN Journal_T.Amount_NU ELSE 0 END) '> 90 DYS'

from Creditor_T,Purchase_T,Journal_T where
Creditor_T.Cred_ID_VC = Purchase_T.Cred_ID_VC and
Purchase_T.Doc_No_VC = Journal_T.Doc_No_VC and
Journal_T.GL_ID = 3000 and
Status_BT = 0

union all

SELECT '','','','','','', 'Total Balance',
SUM(CASE WHEN (GETDATE() - (Purchase_T.Date_DT+Credit_Term_TI))
BETWEEN -100 AND 29.99 THEN Journal_T.Amount_NU ELSE 0 END),
SUM(CASE WHEN (GETDATE() - (Purchase_T.Date_DT+Credit_Term_TI))
BETWEEN 30 AND 59.99 THEN Journal_T.Amount_NU ELSE 0 END),
SUM(CASE WHEN (GETDATE() - (Purchase_T.Date_DT+Credit_Term_TI))
BETWEEN 60 AND 89.99 THEN Journal_T.Amount_NU ELSE 0 END),
SUM(CASE WHEN (GETDATE() - (Purchase_T.Date_DT+Credit_Term_TI))
>= 90 THEN Journal_T.Amount_NU ELSE 0 END)

from Creditor_T,Purchase_T,Journal_T where
Creditor_T.Cred_ID_VC = Purchase_T.Cred_ID_VC and
Purchase_T.Doc_No_VC = Journal_T.Doc_No_VC and
Journal_T.GL_ID = 3000 and
Status_BT = 0
```

Now, test your query, by clicking on the parse query button to check for any syntax error, if your syntax is working, you would see the message "The command(s) completed successfully." If not, go through the code above again, and run the parse query until your syntax is working properly. Then, execute the query, by clicking on the execute query button, and you would see the following output appearing on your result pane.

Creditor...	Inv No	Credit...	Doc No	InvoiceDate	Days Overdue	Due date	Less than 30 DYS	> 30 DYS	> 60 DYS	> 90 DYS
Supplier1	IN100	30	JV1003	20/07/06	464	19/08/06	0	0	0	-300
Supplier1	IN101	30	JV1004	20/07/06	464	19/08/06	0	0	0	-180
Supplier2	IN102	45	JV1005	20/07/06	449	03/09/06	0	0	0	-220
Furniturer1	1257	45	JV1013	20/02/07	234	06/04/07	0	0	0	-1610
		0			0	Total ...	0	0	0	-2310

The above result shows that, all of MaxCorp's creditors have not been paid for more than 90 days.

How It Works – Select Query for Accounts Payable Ageing Report

   Let us analyze the function of our first block of code. Notice that, the select query code has similar coding as the select query we have just created for our stock ageing report. It is basically, the same, as we have utilize the same date function to compute the number of outstanding days for each of the supplier's invoices, based on each invoice's date. We segregate each of the columns by the range of outstanding days computed. We know that all the fields specified, is created in different tables, so we join them together via its common field. We only want to extract those unpaid invoices, therefore we specified the Status as 0.

```
SELECT
 Cred_Name_VC    as    [Creditor    Name],    Inv_ID_VC    as    [Inv    No],
Credit_Term_TI as [Credit Term],Journal_T.Doc_No_VC as [Doc No],
 convert(varchar,Purchase_T.Date_DT,3) as InvoiceDate,
 DATEDIFF(day, Purchase_T.Date_DT+Credit_Term_TI, getdate()) as
 [Days Overdue],
 convert(varchar,DATEADD(day,Credit_Term_TI,Purchase_T.Date_DT),3)as
 Due_date,
 (CASE WHEN (GETDATE() - (Purchase_T.Date_DT+Credit_Term_TI))
 BETWEEN - 100 AND 29.99 THEN Journal_T.Amount_NU ELSE 0 END) AS
 Less_than_30_DYS,
 (CASE WHEN (GETDATE() - (Purchase_T.Date_DT+Credit_Term_TI))
 BETWEEN 30 AND 59.99 THEN Journal_T.Amount_NU ELSE 0 END) AS
 '> 30 DYS',
 (CASE WHEN (GETDATE() - (Purchase_T.Date_DT+Credit_Term_TI))
 BETWEEN 60 AND 89.99 THEN Journal_T.Amount_NU ELSE 0 END) AS
 '> 60 DYS',
 (CASE WHEN (GETDATE() - (Purchase_T.Date_DT+Credit_Term_TI))
 >= 90 THEN Journal_T.Amount_NU ELSE 0 END) '> 90 DYS'

from Creditor_T,Purchase_T,Journal_T where
Creditor_T.Cred_ID_VC = Purchase_T.Cred_ID_VC and
Purchase_T.Doc_No_VC = Journal_T.Doc_No_VC and
Journal_T.GL_ID = 3000 and
Status_BT = 0
```

Then, we sum up a total amount, across all columns, as follows,

```
union all

SELECT '','','','','','', 'Total Balance',
 SUM(CASE WHEN (GETDATE() - (Purchase_T.Date_DT+Credit_Term_TI))
 BETWEEN -100 AND 29.99 THEN Journal_T.Amount_NU ELSE 0 END),
 SUM(CASE WHEN (GETDATE() - (Purchase_T.Date_DT+Credit_Term_TI))
 BETWEEN 30 AND 59.99 THEN Journal_T.Amount_NU ELSE 0 END),
 SUM(CASE WHEN (GETDATE() - (Purchase_T.Date_DT+Credit_Term_TI))
 BETWEEN 60 AND 89.99 THEN Journal_T.Amount_NU ELSE 0 END),
```

```
SUM(CASE WHEN (GETDATE() - (Purchase_T.Date_DT+Credit_Term_TI))
 >= 90 THEN Journal_T.Amount_NU ELSE 0 END)

from Creditor_T,Purchase_T,Journal_T where
Creditor_T.Cred_ID_VC = Purchase_T.Cred_ID_VC and
Purchase_T.Doc_No_VC = Journal_T.Doc_No_VC and
Journal_T.GL_ID = 3000 and
Status_BT = 0
```

2) Using SQL to produce Accounts Payable Payment Status Report

This report would show the payment status of each supplier's invoices. Let us enter the following select query now

```
Select Cred_Name_VC as [Creditor Name],Inv_ID_VC as
 [Inv No],Credit_Term_TI as [Credit Term],
 case when Status_BT = 1 then '$' +
 convert(varchar(22),Journal_T.Amount_NU,100) + ' Paid' else '0' end
as [Invoice Amount]

from Creditor_T,Purchase_T,Journal_T where
Creditor_T.Cred_ID_VC = Purchase_T.Cred_ID_VC and
Purchase_T.Doc_No_VC = Journal_T.Doc_No_VC and
Journal_T.GL_ID = 3000 and
Status_BT = 1

union all

select Cred_Name_VC,Inv_ID_VC,Credit_Term_TI,
 case when Status_BT = 0 then '$' +
 convert(varchar(22),Journal_T.Amount_NU,100) + ' Unpaid' else '0'
end as [Invoice Amount]

from Creditor_T,Purchase_T,Journal_T where
Creditor_T.Cred_ID_VC = Purchase_T.Cred_ID_VC and
Purchase_T.Doc_No_VC = Journal_T.Doc_No_VC and
Journal_T.GL_ID = 3000 and
Status_BT = 0
order by Cred_Name_VC

select 'Total Unpaid' as [Creditors Bal],
 sum(Journal_T.Amount_NU)as [Invoice Amount]

from Creditor_T,Purchase_T,Journal_T where
Creditor_T.Cred_ID_VC = Purchase_T.Cred_ID_VC and
Purchase_T.Doc_No_VC = Journal_T.Doc_No_VC and
Journal_T.GL_ID = 3000 and
Status_BT = 0

union all
```

```
select 'Total paid' as [Creditors Bal],
 sum(Journal_T.Amount_NU)as [Invoice Amount]

from Creditor_T,Purchase_T,Journal_T where
Creditor_T.Cred_ID_VC = Purchase_T.Cred_ID_VC and
Purchase_T.Doc_No_VC = Journal_T.Doc_No_VC and
Journal_T.GL_ID = 3000 and
Status_BT = 1
```

Next, test your query, by clicking on the parse query button to check for any syntax error, if your syntax is working, you would see the message "The command(s) completed successfully." If not, go through the code above again, and run the parse query until your syntax is working properly. Then, execute the query, by clicking on the execute query button, and you would see the following output appearing on your result pane.

	Creditor Name	Inv No	Credit Term	Invoice Amount
1	Furniturer1	1257	45	$-1610 Unpaid
2	Furniturer2	1256	60	$-1710 Paid
3	Supplier1	IN100	30	$-300 Unpaid
4	Supplier1	IN101	30	$-180 Unpaid
5	Supplier2	IN102	45	$-220 Unpaid

	Creditors Bal	Invoice Amount
1	Total Unpaid	-2310
2	Total paid	-1710

Above report shows Dave, that, a total of $2,310, is still unpaid to its respective supplier, which is the same amount, reflected on the Accounts Payable ageing report, we have created previously.

How It Works – Select Query for Payable Payment Status Report

Let us go through our first block of code. We select the creditor name in our first column, then its invoices on the second column, next its credit term, and the amount. Notice, here, we use the conversion function, to convert our numerical data type to a variable character type, in order for us, to concatenate the word 'Paid' and the '$' symbol to appear as characters on our result pane. We will first select those records, with the status of 1, as our first output, next those with the status of 0, and we join the results together using the union all clause. We know all the specified fields are created from three different tables, so we join these three tables together in our select query.

```
Select Cred_Name_VC as [Creditor Name],Inv_ID_VC as
 [Inv No],Credit_Term_TI as [Credit Term],
 case when Status_BT = 1 then '$' +
 convert(varchar(22),Journal_T.Amount_NU,100) + ' Paid' else '0' end
as [Invoice Amount]

from Creditor_T,Purchase_T,Journal_T where
Creditor_T.Cred_ID_VC = Purchase_T.Cred_ID_VC and
Purchase_T.Doc_No_VC = Journal_T.Doc_No_VC and
Journal_T.GL_ID = 3000 and
Status_BT = 1

union all

select Cred_Name_VC,Inv_ID_VC,Credit_Term_TI,
 case when Status_BT = 0 then '$' +
 convert(varchar(22),Journal_T.Amount_NU,100) + ' Unpaid' else '0'
end as [Invoice Amount]

from Creditor_T,Purchase_T,Journal_T where
Creditor_T.Cred_ID_VC = Purchase_T.Cred_ID_VC and
Purchase_T.Doc_No_VC = Journal_T.Doc_No_VC and
Journal_T.GL_ID = 3000 and
Status_BT = 0
order by Cred_Name_VC
```

Summary

In Chapter 10, we have learned how to create reports from the Purchase Table, applying the Transact-SQL to perform the select query to produce the necessary accounting reports required by MaxCorp.

To summarize, in this chapter, we have discussed:

> ➢ How to create select query to produce an Accounts Payable Ageing Report

> ➢ How to create select query to produce an Accounts Payable Payment Status Report

Chapter 11

Creating Reports from Sales Table

In our earlier chapter, we have gone through the process of creating and normalising the Sale Table and Dave have once again, requested the following reports to be created from the Sale Table.

1) Accounts Receivable Ageing Report
2) Accounts Receivable Collection Status Report
3) Sales Analysis Report

1) Using SQL to produce Accounts Receivable Ageing Report

This report would produce the similar ageing report we have created from the Purchase Table. This report would show the ageing of each invoices issued to each customer, in days.

Let us enter the following test data, as follows,

Sale_T

Cust_ID_VC	Pdt_ID_VC	Doc_No_VC	Date_DT	Status_BT	Inv_ID_VC
CUST100	1235	JV1000	39214	1	INV100
CUST101	1234	JV1001	39316	1	INV102
CUST102	1234	JV1002	39236	0	INV103

Customer_T

Cust_ID_VC	Cust_Name_VC	Cust_Add_VC	Cust_Contact_VC	Credit_Term_TI	Cust_Code_VC
CUST100	William	44th Avenue	7879888	30	2003
CUST101	Randy	12th Solroda	121211	45	2003
CUST102	Hulete	11th Palm Beach	455454	60	2003

Now, enter the following select query as follows:

```
SELECT Cust_Name_VC as [Customer Name],Inv_ID_VC as
 [Inv No],Credit_Term_TI as [Credit Term],
 convert(varchar,Sale_T.Date_DT,3) as InvoiceDate,
 DATEDIFF(day, Sale_T.Date_DT+Credit_Term_TI, getdate()) as
 [Days Overdue],
 convert(varchar,DATEADD(day, Credit_Term_TI, Sale_T.Date_DT),3)as
 Due_date,

 (CASE WHEN (GETDATE() - (Sale_T.Date_DT+Credit_Term_TI)) BETWEEN
 -100 AND 29.99
 THEN Amount_NU ELSE 0 END) AS '< 30 DYS',
```

```
(CASE WHEN (GETDATE() - (Sale_T.Date_DT+Credit_Term_TI)) BETWEEN
 30 AND 59.99 THEN Amount_NU ELSE 0 END) AS '> 30 DYS',
(CASE WHEN (GETDATE() - (Sale_T.Date_DT+Credit_Term_TI)) >= 60
 THEN Amount_NU ELSE 0 END) '> 60 DYS'

from Customer_T,Sale_T,Journal_T
where Customer_T.Cust_ID_VC = Sale_T.Cust_ID_VC
and Journal_T.Doc_No_VC = Sale_T.Doc_No_VC
and Journal_T.GL_ID = 2003
and Sale_T.Status_BT = 0

union all

SELECT '','',0,'',0, 'Total Balance',
 SUM(CASE WHEN (GETDATE() - (Sale_T.Date_DT+Credit_Term_TI)) BETWEEN
 -100 AND 29.99 THEN Amount_NU ELSE 0 END),
 SUM(CASE WHEN (GETDATE() - (Sale_T.Date_DT+Credit_Term_TI)) BETWEEN
 30 AND 59.99 THEN Amount_NU ELSE 0 END),
 SUM(CASE WHEN (GETDATE() - (Sale_T.Date_DT+Credit_Term_TI))
 >= 60 THEN Amount_NU ELSE 0 END)

from Customer_T,Sale_T,Journal_T
where Customer_T.Cust_ID_VC = Sale_T.Cust_ID_VC
and Journal_T.Doc_No_VC = Sale_T.Doc_No_VC
and Journal_T.GL_ID = 2003
and Sale_T.Status_BT = 0
```

Now, Test your query, by clicking on the parse query button to check for any syntax error, if your syntax is working, you would see the message "The command(s) completed successfully." If not, go through the code above again, and run the parse query until your syntax is working properly. Then, execute the query, by clicking on the execute query button, and you would see the following output appearing on your result pane.

Customer Name	Inv No	Credit Term	InvoiceDate	Days Overdue	Due_date	< 30 DYS	> 30 DYS	> 60 DYS
Hulete	INV103	60	03/06/07	116	02/08/07	0	0	2500
		0		0	Total Balance	0	0	2500

As shown on the above result pane, MaxCorp only has one uncollected debt from a customer that is overdue for more than 60 days, judging from its invoice date.

How It Works – Select Query for Accounts Receivable Ageing Report

Let us try to understand the function on our first block of code. On the first column, we select the customer name; follow by its invoice number, credit terms, invoice date and amount. Here, again, we apply the date function, to change the current date format to our required format, and we place the outstanding amount on the right ageing period. We only want to pull records from the debtor code, so we specify the account code, 2003, with status 0. We know that, the required fields are all created from different tables, so we join the Customer Table, the Sale Table, and the Journal Table together via its common field.

```sql
SELECT Cust_Name_VC as [Customer Name],Inv_ID_VC as
 [Inv No],Credit_Term_TI as [Credit Term],
 convert(varchar,Sale_T.Date_DT,3) as InvoiceDate,
 DATEDIFF(day, Sale_T.Date_DT+Credit_Term_TI, getdate()) as
 [Days Overdue],
 convert(varchar,DATEADD(day, Credit_Term_TI, Sale_T.Date_DT),3)as
 Due_date,
 (CASE WHEN (GETDATE() - (Sale_T.Date_DT+Credit_Term_TI)) BETWEEN
  -100 AND 29.99 THEN Amount_NU ELSE 0 END) AS '< 30 DYS',
 (CASE WHEN (GETDATE() - (Sale_T.Date_DT+Credit_Term_TI)) BETWEEN
  30 AND 59.99 THEN Amount_NU ELSE 0 END) AS '> 30 DYS',
 (CASE WHEN (GETDATE() - (Sale_T.Date_DT+Credit_Term_TI))
  >= 60 THEN Amount_NU ELSE 0 END) '> 60 DYS'

from Customer_T,Sale_T,Journal_T
where Customer_T.Cust_ID_VC = Sale_T.Cust_ID_VC
and Journal_T.Doc_No_VC = Sale_T.Doc_No_VC
and Journal_T.GL_ID = 2003
and Sale_T.Status_BT = 0
```

Next, we sum up all the ageing period, across all columns with numerical output, and place them under the total balance row.

```sql
union all

SELECT '','',0,'',0, 'Total Balance',
 SUM(CASE WHEN (GETDATE() - (Sale_T.Date_DT+Credit_Term_TI)) BETWEEN
 -100 AND 29.99 THEN Amount_NU ELSE 0 END),
 SUM(CASE WHEN (GETDATE() - (Sale_T.Date_DT+Credit_Term_TI)) BETWEEN
 30 AND 59.99 THEN Amount_NU ELSE 0 END),
 SUM(CASE WHEN (GETDATE() - (Sale_T.Date_DT+Credit_Term_TI))
 >= 60 THEN Amount_NU ELSE 0 END)

from Customer_T,Sale_T,Journal_T
where Customer_T.Cust_ID_VC = Sale_T.Cust_ID_VC
and Journal_T.Doc_No_VC = Sale_T.Doc_No_VC
and Journal_T.GL_ID = 2003
and Sale_T.Status_BT = 0
```

2) Using SQL to produce Accounts Receivable Collection Status Report

This report will show the collection status of MaxCorp's customer, as what we have created similarly for the Accounts Payable Payment Status report from the Purchase Table.

Now, enter the following select query, as follows:

```
select Cust_Name_VC as [Customer Name],Inv_ID_VC as [Inv No],
Credit_Term_TI as [Credit Term],case when Status_BT = 1
then '$' + convert(varchar(22),Amount_NU,100)
 + ' Paid' else '0' end as [Invoice Amount]

from Customer_T,Sale_T,Journal_T
where Customer_T.Cust_ID_VC = Sale_T.Cust_ID_VC
and Journal_T.Doc_No_VC = Sale_T.Doc_No_VC
and Journal_T.GL_ID = 2003
and Sale_T.Status_BT = 1

union all

select Cust_Name_VC,Inv_ID_VC,Credit_Term_TI,
 case when Status_BT = 0
then '$' + convert(varchar(22),Amount_NU,100)
 + ' Unpaid' else '0' end as [Invoice Amount]

from Customer_T,Sale_T,Journal_T
where Customer_T.Cust_ID_VC = Sale_T.Cust_ID_VC
and Journal_T.Doc_No_VC = Sale_T.Doc_No_VC
and Journal_T.GL_ID = 2003
and Sale_T.Status_BT = 0
order by Cust_Name_VC
```

Now, try testing your query, by clicking on the parse query button to check for any syntax error, if your syntax is working, you would see the message "The command(s) completed successfully." If not, go through the code above again, and run the parse query until your syntax is working properly. Then, execute the query, by clicking on the execute query button, and you would see the following output appearing on your result pane.

	Customer Name	Inv No	Credit Term	Invoice Amount
1	Hulete	INV103	60	$2500 Unpaid
2	Randy	INV102	45	$2000 Paid
3	William	INV100	30	$2000 Paid

Base on the above report, we found out, that MaxCorp has only one uncollected debt from a customer, as what was shown on the Accounts Receivable Ageing report above.

How It Works – Select Query for Accounts Receivable Collection Status Report

Let us go through the function of our select query. We select the customer name, to appear on the first column, next its invoice number, credit term, and its corresponding amount, converting its current numerical type, to a character type, and concatenate it with the word 'Paid' and the symbol '$' as a combined character. We know that all these fields are created from different tables, so, we join these tables together, in order for us to pull the relevant records from the respective fields.

```
select Cust_Name_VC as [Customer Name],Inv_ID_VC as
 [Inv No],Credit_Term_TI as [Credit Term],
 case when Status_BT = 1
then '$' + convert(varchar(22),Amount_NU,100)
 + ' Paid' else '0' end as [Invoice Amount]

from Customer_T,Sale_T,Journal_T
where Customer_T.Cust_ID_VC = Sale_T.Cust_ID_VC
and Journal_T.Doc_No_VC = Sale_T.Doc_No_VC
and Journal_T.GL_ID = 2003
and Sale_T.Status_BT = 1
```

We also want to pull records for those customers who have not paid to MaxCorp, so we repeat our query as the above, specifying the status 0 and join the filtering result together with our first result, using the union all clause. We also want to sort our result, by customer name, so we specify this in the order by clause on our last query.

```
union all

select Cust_Name_VC,Inv_ID_VC,Credit_Term_TI,
 case when Status_BT = 0
then '$' + convert(varchar(22),Amount_NU,100)
 + ' Unpaid' else '0' end as [Invoice Amount]

from Customer_T,Sale_T,Journal_T
where Customer_T.Cust_ID_VC = Sale_T.Cust_ID_VC
and Journal_T.Doc_No_VC = Sale_T.Doc_No_VC
and Journal_T.GL_ID = 2003
and Sale_T.Status_BT = 0
order by Cust_Name_VC
```

3) Using SQL to produce Sales Analysis Report

This report would show, Dave, how much gross profit, MaxCorp is making out of each sale made in year 2007, by product type. First, we will enter the following test data in the following table:

Product_Category_T		
Pdt_Category_VC	Category_Name_VC	GL_ID
PDT100	Software	5002
PDT100	Software	6002
PDT101	Hardware	5001
PDT101	Hardware	6001

Next, enter the following select query as follows:

```
select Category_Name_VC as [Product Type],Inv_ID_VC as
 [Inv No],Cust_Name_VC as [Cust_Name],
 convert(varchar(08),Journal_T.Date_DT,3) as [Invoice
 Date],Journal_T.Descrip_VC as [Description],
 Journal_T.Amount_NU as [Sales],
 Stock_Movement_T.Qty_NU  *  Stock_Movement_T.Unit_Price_TI*-1  as
[Cost],Journal_T.Amount_NU - (Stock_Movement_T.Qty_NU *
 Stock_Movement_T.Unit_Price_TI)  as [GP],
 convert(decimal,((Journal_T.Amount_NU - (Stock_Movement_T.Qty_NU *
 Stock_Movement_T.Unit_Price_TI))/Journal_T.Amount_NU * 100),2) as
 [GP%]

from Stock_Movement_T,Journal_T,Product_Category_T,Customer_T,Sale_T
where
Customer_T.Cust_ID_VC = Sale_T.Cust_ID_VC and
Sale_T.Doc_No_VC = Stock_Movement_T.Doc_No_VC and
Stock_Movement_T.Doc_No_VC = Journal_T.Doc_No_VC and
Journal_T.GL_ID = Product_Category_T.GL_ID and
Journal_T.GL_ID IN (5001,5002) and Journal_T.Year_SI = 2007

union all

select '','','','','Total',
 sum(case when Journal_T.GL_ID in ('5001','5002') and
 Journal_T.Year_SI = 2007 then Journal_T.Amount_NU else 0 end),
 sum(case when Journal_T.GL_ID in ('6001','6002') and
 Journal_T.Year_SI = 2007 then Journal_T.Amount_NU else 0 end),
 sum(case when Journal_T.GL_ID in ('5001','5002') and
 Journal_T.Year_SI = 2007 then Journal_T.Amount_NU else 0 end) +
 sum(case    when    Journal_T.GL_ID    in    ('6001','6002')    and
Journal_T.Year_SI = 2007 then Journal_T.Amount_NU else 0 end),0

from Journal_T
```

Let us run your query, by clicking on the parse query button to check for any syntax error, if your syntax is working, you would see the message "The command(s) completed successfully." If not, go through the code above again, and run the parse query until your syntax is working properly. Then, execute the query, by clicking on the execute query button, and you would see the following result appearing on your result pane.

	Product Type	Inv No	Cust_Name	Invoice Date	Description	Sales	Cost	GP	GP%
1	Hardware	INV100	William	12/05/07	HP Presario-TX 101 P4	-2000	150	-1850	93
2	Hardware	INV102	Randy	22/08/07	HP Presario-TX 101 P4	-2000	150	-1850	93
3	Software	INV103	Hulete	03/06/07	Red Hat-version 2.0	-2500	100	-2400	96
4					Total	-6500	400	-6100	0

The report shows that, MaxCorp's main contribution is from its software sale, having a GP of 96%.

How It Works – Select Query for Sales Analysis Report

Now, let us run through our select query we have just created for the sales analysis report. We select the product type to appear on our first column, then, its invoice number, next, its customer name, invoice date, and its description from various table quoted on the below syntax, by matching its year to be 2007, and having the account code of 5001 and 5002.We then select the sale amount from the journal table, the cost of sale, by multiplying the units against its unit price, drawing the details from the Stock_Movement Table. Next, we compute the gross profit, to be the difference between the sales and its cost of sales amount. We compute the gross profit percentage, by multiplying our gross profit with the value of 100, converting the output to the nearest 2 decimal point. We then combine all the relevant tables via its common fields, in order to allow us to extract the relevant records from their respective fields.

```
select Category_Name_VC as [Product Type],Inv_ID_VC as
 [Inv No],Cust_Name_VC as [Cust_Name],
 convert(varchar(08),Journal_T.Date_DT,3) as [Invoice
 Date],Journal_T.Descrip_VC as [Description],
 Journal_T.Amount_NU as [Sales],
 Stock_Movement_T.Qty_NU  *  Stock_Movement_T.Unit_Price_TI*-1  as
[Cost],Journal_T.Amount_NU - (Stock_Movement_T.Qty_NU *
 Stock_Movement_T.Unit_Price_TI)  as [GP],
 convert(decimal,((Journal_T.Amount_NU - (Stock_Movement_T.Qty_NU *
 Stock_Movement_T.Unit_Price_TI))/Journal_T.Amount_NU * 100),2) as
 [GP%]

from Stock_Movement_T,Journal_T,Product_Category_T,Customer_T,Sale_T
where
```

```
Customer_T.Cust_ID_VC = Sale_T.Cust_ID_VC and
Sale_T.Doc_No_VC = Stock_Movement_T.Doc_No_VC and
Stock_Movement_T.Doc_No_VC = Journal_T.Doc_No_VC and
Journal_T.GL_ID = Product_Category_T.GL_ID and
Journal_T.GL_ID IN (5001,5002) and
Journal_T.Year_SI = 2007
```

We then, join the above result with the below result using the 'union all' clause. The query below will create a row, totaling up the sales, cost, and gross profit amount. This time, we only extract from one table only, the Journal Table.

```
union all

select '','','','','Total',
 sum(case when Journal_T.GL_ID in ('5001','5002') and
 Journal_T.Year_SI = 2007 then Journal_T.Amount_NU else 0 end),
 sum(case when Journal_T.GL_ID in ('6001','6002') and
 Journal_T.Year_SI = 2007 then Journal_T.Amount_NU else 0 end),
 sum(case when Journal_T.GL_ID in ('5001','5002') and
 Journal_T.Year_SI = 2007 then Journal_T.Amount_NU else 0 end) +
 sum(case    when    Journal_T.GL_ID    in    ('6001','6002')    and
Journal_T.Year_SI = 2007 then Journal_T.Amount_NU else 0 end),0

from Journal_T
```

Summary

In Chapter 11, we have learned how to create reports from the Sale Table, applying the Transact-SQL to perform the select query to produce the necessary accounting reports required by MaxCorp.

To summarize, in this chapter, we have discussed:

➢ How to create select query to produce an Accounts Receivable Ageing Report

➢ How to create select query to produce an AR Collection Status Report

➢ How to create select query to produce Sales Analysis Report

Chapter 12

Creating Reports from Cash Table

This is an important Table, as it contains cash flow details performed by MaxCorp and Dave have requested some special reports to be created from this table, as he has pointed out, when we were discussing how to create the Cash Table in Chapter 6. Let us look at some of the reports that he has mentioned earlier.

1) Cash Flow Forecast
2) Cash Flow Summary Statement (Direct Method)
3) Cash Flow Periodic Statement (Direct Method)
4) Bank Reconciliation Statement

1) Using SQL to produce Cash Flow Forecast

This report would show the Cash inflow and outflow of all MaxCorp's due collection and payment. The inflow from customer would be computed based on the last day of its credit term given to each sales invoice. Likewise, the outflow to supplier, would be computed based on the last day of its credit term stated on each purchase invoices.

Enter the following test data into the Cash Table as shown below:

Cash_T				
Doc_No_VC	Cash_Type_VC	Cash_Category_VC	Chq_No_VC	Bank_Code_VC
JV1017	OA	OA_Int	745570	CITI
JV1018	OA	OA_Tax	745571	CITI
JV1019	IA	IA_Int	44511	CITI
JV1020	FA	FA_Cap	8875	CITI
JV1021	IA	IA_Pur	745571	CITI
JV1022	OA	OA_Deb	95454	CITI
JV1023	OA	OA_Deb	12454	CITI

Next, let us enter the following select query as follows

```
select Descrip_VC as [Collection Forecast],
 Journal_T.Doc_No_VC as [Doc No],Cust_Name_VC as [Customer Name],
 sum(case when MONTH(Sale_T.Date_DT+Customer_T.Credit_Term_TI)
 BETWEEN 0 AND 1
 then Journal_T.Amount_NU else 0 end) as [Period 01],
 sum(case when MONTH(Sale_T.Date_DT+Customer_T.Credit_Term_TI)
 BETWEEN 1.99 AND 2
```

```
     then Journal_T.Amount_NU else 0 end) as [Period 02],
     sum(case when MONTH(Sale_T.Date_DT+Customer_T.Credit_Term_TI)
     BETWEEN 2.99 AND 3
     then Journal_T.Amount_NU else 0 end) as [Period 03],
     sum(case when MONTH(Sale_T.Date_DT+Customer_T.Credit_Term_TI)
     BETWEEN 3.99 AND 4
     then Journal_T.Amount_NU else 0 end) as [Period 04],
     sum(case when MONTH(Sale_T.Date_DT+Customer_T.Credit_Term_TI)
     BETWEEN 4.99 AND 5
     then Journal_T.Amount_NU else 0 end) as [Period 05],
     sum(case when MONTH(Sale_T.Date_DT+Customer_T.Credit_Term_TI)
     BETWEEN 5.99 AND 6
     then Journal_T.Amount_NU else 0 end) as [Period 06],
     sum(case when MONTH(Sale_T.Date_DT+Customer_T.Credit_Term_TI)
     BETWEEN 6.99 AND 7
     then Journal_T.Amount_NU else 0 end) as [Period 07],
     sum(case when MONTH(Sale_T.Date_DT+Customer_T.Credit_Term_TI)
     BETWEEN 7.99 AND 8
     then Journal_T.Amount_NU else 0 end) as [Period 08],
     sum(case when MONTH(Sale_T.Date_DT+Customer_T.Credit_Term_TI)
     BETWEEN 8.99 AND 9
     then Journal_T.Amount_NU else 0 end) as [Period 09],
     sum(case when MONTH(Sale_T.Date_DT+Customer_T.Credit_Term_TI)
     BETWEEN 9.99 AND 10
     then Journal_T.Amount_NU else 0 end) as [Period 10],
     sum(case when MONTH(Sale_T.Date_DT+Customer_T.Credit_Term_TI)
     BETWEEN 10.99 AND 11
     then Journal_T.Amount_NU else 0 end) as [Period 11],
     sum(case when MONTH(Sale_T.Date_DT+Customer_T.Credit_Term_TI)
     BETWEEN 11.99 AND 12
     then Journal_T.Amount_NU else 0 end) as [Period 12]

from Customer_T,Sale_T,Journal_T
where
Customer_T.Cust_ID_VC = Sale_T.Cust_ID_VC and
Sale_T.Doc_No_VC = Journal_T.Doc_No_VC
and Journal_T.GL_ID = 2003
and Status_BT = 0
group by Descrip_VC,Journal_T.Doc_No_VC,Cust_Name_VC

union all

select 'Total Collection Forecast','','',
     sum(case when MONTH(Sale_T.Date_DT+Customer_T.Credit_Term_TI)
     BETWEEN 0 AND 1
     then Journal_T.Amount_NU else 0 end) as [Period 01],
     sum(case when MONTH(Sale_T.Date_DT+Customer_T.Credit_Term_TI)
     BETWEEN 1.99 AND 2
     then Journal_T.Amount_NU else 0 end) as [Period 02],
     sum(case when MONTH(Sale_T.Date_DT+Customer_T.Credit_Term_TI)
     BETWEEN 2.99 AND 3
     then Journal_T.Amount_NU else 0 end) as [Period 03],
```

```sql
sum(case when MONTH(Sale_T.Date_DT+Customer_T.Credit_Term_TI)
BETWEEN 3.99 AND 4
then Journal_T.Amount_NU else 0 end) as [Period 04],
sum(case when MONTH(Sale_T.Date_DT+Customer_T.Credit_Term_TI)
BETWEEN 4.99 AND 5
then Journal_T.Amount_NU else 0 end) as [Period 05],
sum(case when MONTH(Sale_T.Date_DT+Customer_T.Credit_Term_TI)
BETWEEN 5.99 AND 6
then Journal_T.Amount_NU else 0 end) as [Period 06],
sum(case when MONTH(Sale_T.Date_DT+Customer_T.Credit_Term_TI)
BETWEEN 6.99 AND 7
then Journal_T.Amount_NU else 0 end) as [Period 07],
sum(case when MONTH(Sale_T.Date_DT+Customer_T.Credit_Term_TI)
BETWEEN 7.99 AND 8
then Journal_T.Amount_NU else 0 end) as [Period 08],
sum(case when MONTH(Sale_T.Date_DT+Customer_T.Credit_Term_TI)
BETWEEN  8.99 AND 9
then Journal_T.Amount_NU else 0 end) as [Period 09],
sum(case when MONTH(Sale_T.Date_DT+Customer_T.Credit_Term_TI)
BETWEEN 9.99 AND 10
then Journal_T.Amount_NU else 0 end) as [Period 10],
sum(case when MONTH(Sale_T.Date_DT+Customer_T.Credit_Term_TI)
BETWEEN 10.99 AND 11
then Journal_T.Amount_NU else 0 end) as [Period 11],
sum(case when MONTH(Sale_T.Date_DT+Customer_T.Credit_Term_TI)
BETWEEN 11.99 AND 12
then Journal_T.Amount_NU else 0 end) as [Period 12]

from Customer_T,Sale_T,Journal_T
where
Customer_T.Cust_ID_VC = Sale_T.Cust_ID_VC and
Sale_T.Doc_No_VC = Journal_T.Doc_No_VC
and Journal_T.GL_ID = 2003
and Status_BT = 0

select Descrip_VC as [Payment Forecast],
 Journal_T.Doc_No_VC as [Doc No],Cred_Name_VC as [Creditor Name],
 sum(case when MONTH(Purchase_T.Date_DT+Creditor_T.Credit_Term_TI)
 BETWEEN 0 AND 1
 then Journal_T.Amount_NU else 0 end) as [Period 01],
 sum(case when MONTH(Purchase_T.Date_DT+Creditor_T.Credit_Term_TI)
 BETWEEN 1.99 AND 2
 then Journal_T.Amount_NU else 0 end) as [Period 02],
 sum(case when MONTH(Purchase_T.Date_DT+Creditor_T.Credit_Term_TI)
 BETWEEN 2.99 AND 3
 then Journal_T.Amount_NU else 0 end) as [Period 03],

 sum(case when MONTH(Purchase_T.Date_DT+Creditor_T.Credit_Term_TI)
 BETWEEN 3.99 AND 4
 then Journal_T.Amount_NU else 0 end) as [Period 04],
 sum(case when MONTH(Purchase_T.Date_DT+Creditor_T.Credit_Term_TI)
 BETWEEN 4.99 AND 5
```

```sql
       then Journal_T.Amount_NU else 0 end) as [Period 05],
    sum(case when MONTH(Purchase_T.Date_DT+Creditor_T.Credit_Term_TI)
    BETWEEN 5.99 AND 6
    then Journal_T.Amount_NU else 0 end) as [Period 06],
    sum(case when MONTH(Purchase_T.Date_DT+Creditor_T.Credit_Term_TI)
    BETWEEN 6.99 AND 7
    then Journal_T.Amount_NU else 0 end) as [Period 07],
    sum(case when MONTH(Purchase_T.Date_DT+Creditor_T.Credit_Term_TI)
    BETWEEN 7.99 AND 8
    then Journal_T.Amount_NU else 0 end) as [Period 08],
    sum(case when MONTH(Purchase_T.Date_DT+Creditor_T.Credit_Term_TI)
    BETWEEN 8.99 AND 9
    then Journal_T.Amount_NU else 0 end) as [Period 09],
    sum(case when MONTH(Purchase_T.Date_DT+Creditor_T.Credit_Term_TI)
    BETWEEN 9.99 AND 10
    then Journal_T.Amount_NU else 0 end) as [Period 10],
    sum(case when MONTH(Purchase_T.Date_DT+Creditor_T.Credit_Term_TI)
    BETWEEN 10.99 AND 11
    then Journal_T.Amount_NU else 0 end) as [Period 11],
    sum(case when MONTH(Purchase_T.Date_DT+Creditor_T.Credit_Term_TI)
    BETWEEN 11.99 AND 12
    then Journal_T.Amount_NU else 0 end) as [Period 12]

from Creditor_T,Purchase_T,Journal_T
where
Creditor_T.Cred_ID_VC = Purchase_T.Cred_ID_VC and
Purchase_T.Doc_No_VC = Journal_T.Doc_No_VC
and Journal_T.GL_ID = 3000
and Status_BT = 0
group by Descrip_VC,Journal_T.Doc_No_VC,Cred_Name_VC

union all

select 'Total Payment Forecast','','',
    sum(case when MONTH(Purchase_T.Date_DT+Creditor_T.Credit_Term_TI)
    BETWEEN 0 AND 1
    then Journal_T.Amount_NU else 0 end) as [Period 01],
    sum(case when MONTH(Purchase_T.Date_DT+Creditor_T.Credit_Term_TI)
    BETWEEN 1.99 AND 2
    then Journal_T.Amount_NU else 0 end) as [Period 02],
    sum(case when MONTH(Purchase_T.Date_DT+Creditor_T.Credit_Term_TI)
    BETWEEN 2.99 AND 3
    then Journal_T.Amount_NU else 0 end) as [Period 03],
    sum(case when MONTH(Purchase_T.Date_DT+Creditor_T.Credit_Term_TI)
    BETWEEN 3.99 AND 4
    then Journal_T.Amount_NU else 0 end) as [Period 04],
    sum(case when MONTH(Purchase_T.Date_DT+Creditor_T.Credit_Term_TI)
    BETWEEN 4.99 AND 5
    then Journal_T.Amount_NU else 0 end) as [Period 05],

    sum(case when MONTH(Purchase_T.Date_DT+Creditor_T.Credit_Term_TI)
    BETWEEN 5.99 AND 6
```

```
then Journal_T.Amount_NU else 0 end) as [Period 06],
sum(case when MONTH(Purchase_T.Date_DT+Creditor_T.Credit_Term_TI)
BETWEEN 6.99 AND 7
then Journal_T.Amount_NU else 0 end) as [Period 07],
sum(case when MONTH(Purchase_T.Date_DT+Creditor_T.Credit_Term_TI)
BETWEEN 7.99 AND 8
then Journal_T.Amount_NU else 0 end) as [Period 08],
sum(case when MONTH(Purchase_T.Date_DT+Creditor_T.Credit_Term_TI)
BETWEEN 8.99 AND 9
then Journal_T.Amount_NU else 0 end) as [Period 09],
sum(case when MONTH(Purchase_T.Date_DT+Creditor_T.Credit_Term_TI)
BETWEEN 9.99 AND 10
then Journal_T.Amount_NU else 0 end) as [Period 10],
sum(case when MONTH(Purchase_T.Date_DT+Creditor_T.Credit_Term_TI)
BETWEEN 10.99 AND 11
then Journal_T.Amount_NU else 0 end) as [Period 11],
sum(case when MONTH(Purchase_T.Date_DT+Creditor_T.Credit_Term_TI)
BETWEEN 11.99 AND 12
then Journal_T.Amount_NU else 0 end) as [Period 12]

from Creditor_T,Purchase_T,Journal_T
where
Creditor_T.Cred_ID_VC = Purchase_T.Cred_ID_VC and
Purchase_T.Doc_No_VC = Journal_T.Doc_No_VC
and Journal_T.GL_ID = 3000
and Status_BT = 0
```

Now, try testing your query, by clicking on the parse query button to check for any syntax error, if your syntax is working, you would see the message "The command(s) completed successfully." If not, go through the code above again, and run the parse query until your syntax is working properly. Then, execute the query, by clicking on the execute query button, and you would see the following output appearing on your result pane.

Collection Forecast	Doc No	Customer Name	Period 01	Period 02	Period 03	Period 04	Period 05	Period 06
Red Hat-version 2.0	JV1002	Hulete	0	0	0	0	0	0
Total Collection Forecast			0	0	0	0	0	0

Payment Forecast	Doc No	Creditor Name	Period 01	Period 02	Period 03	Period 04	Period 05	Period 06
HP Presario-TX 101 P4	JV1003	Supplier1	0	0	0	0	0	0
HP Presario-TX 101 P4	JV1004	Supplier1	0	0	0	0	0	0
Purchase FA	JV1013	Furniturer1	0	0	0	-1610	0	0
Red Hat-version 2.0	JV1005	Supplier2	0	0	0	0	0	0
Total Payment Forecast			0	0	0	-1610	0	0

You should be able to see the result as shown above, after executing your select query. As what we have seen here, MaxCorp would have $1610 due for payment on period 4, and an outstanding debt of $2,500 due for collection on period 8.

How It Works – Select Query for Cash Flow Forecast Report

Let us run through our first block of code now. We start, by extracting the description to be on our first column, next, the document number, customer name, and subsequently, we compute the last due days of each invoices, and place them on the right month. We will compute this for all twelve months. We call our query to apply the date function again, to add on the credit term to each invoice date, and then, we convert the maturing period from days to month, and place them on period 01 column, if the maturity is between 0 and 1st month. We continue to do the same for the remaining periods.

We know that, all the fieldname specified in our query, is created from different table, so we join all the three tables together, in order to pull the records that we want. Remember, we only want to extract those from the debtor code, so, we filter by account code, 2003, and with the unpaid status 0.

```
select Descrip_VC as [Collection Forecast],
 Journal_T.Doc_No_VC as [Doc No],Cust_Name_VC as [Customer Name],
 sum(case when MONTH(Sale_T.Date_DT+Customer_T.Credit_Term_TI)
 BETWEEN 0 AND 1 then Journal_T.Amount_NU else 0 end) as [Period
01],

    ..............................................................................
    .............................................................................

 sum(case when MONTH(Sale_T.Date_DT+Customer_T.Credit_Term_TI)
 BETWEEN 11.99 AND 12
 then Journal_T.Amount_NU else 0 end) as [Period 12]

from Customer_T,Sale_T,Journal_T
where
Customer_T.Cust_ID_VC = Sale_T.Cust_ID_VC and
Sale_T.Doc_No_VC = Journal_T.Doc_No_VC
and Journal_T.GL_ID = 2003
and Status_BT = 0
group by Descrip_VC,Journal_T.Doc_No_VC,Cust_Name_VC
```

Next, we join our result above, with the subtotal result, using the union all clause that we have created from the following query.

```
union all

select 'Total Collection Forecast','','',
 sum(case when MONTH(Sale_T.Date_DT+Customer_T.Credit_Term_TI)
 BETWEEN 0 AND 1
 then Journal_T.Amount_NU else 0 end) as [Period 01],
..................................................................................
.................................................................................
```

```
sum(case when MONTH(Sale_T.Date_DT+Customer_T.Credit_Term_TI)
 BETWEEN 11.99 AND 12
 then Journal_T.Amount_NU else 0 end) as [Period 12]

from Customer_T, Sale_T, Journal_T
where
Customer_T.Cust_ID_VC = Sale_T.Cust_ID_VC and
Sale_T.Doc_No_VC = Journal_T.Doc_No_VC
and Journal_T.GL_ID = 2003
and Status_BT = 0
```

As for the query created for creditor payment forecast, its function is basically the same as the one we have created for the customer collection forecast, except that, we replace the account code with the creditor code of 3000 and replacing the Sale and Customer Table with Purchase and Creditor Table.

2) Using SQL to produce Cash Flow Summary Statement

This report would actually show Dave, how MaxCorp's cash has been utilized in a year, categorizing its type of cash inflow and outflow, into three main categories, operating activities, investing activities and financing activities. The reason why, it is known as a direct method, is because, the cash flow is pulling directly from its source, namely, from its debtor and creditor accounts. We shall understand this more, when we create and execute the following select query.

Let us enter the following select query

```
select 'Cash from Operating Activities :' as [Cash Flow Statement],
 sum(case when Cash_Type_VC = 'aaa' then Journal_T.Amount_NU else
 0 end) as [$]

from Cash_T join Journal_T on
Cash_T.Doc_No_VC = Journal_T.Doc_No_VC

union all

select 'Cash receipt from Customer',
 sum(case when Cash_Type_VC = 'OA' and Cash_Category_VC = 'OA_Deb'
and Year_SI = 2007 and GL_ID = 2002
 then Journal_T.Amount_NU else 0 end)

from Cash_T join Journal_T on
Cash_T.Doc_No_VC = Journal_T.Doc_No_VC
```

```
union all

select 'Cash paid to Supplier',
 sum(case when Cash_Type_VC = 'OA' and Cash_Category_VC = 'OA_Sup'
and Year_SI = 2007 and GL_ID = 2002
 then Journal_T.Amount_NU else 0 end)

from Cash_T join Journal_T on
Cash_T.Doc_No_VC = Journal_T.Doc_No_VC

union all

select 'Cash generated from Operations',
 sum(case when Cash_Type_VC = 'OA' and Cash_Category_VC = 'OA_Deb'
and Year_SI = 2007 and GL_ID = 2002
 then Journal_T.Amount_NU else 0 end) +
 sum(case when Cash_Type_VC = 'OA' and Cash_Category_VC = 'OA_Sup'
and Year_SI = 2007 and GL_ID = 2002
 then Journal_T.Amount_NU else 0 end)

from Cash_T join Journal_T on
Cash_T.Doc_No_VC = Journal_T.Doc_No_VC

union all

select 'Interest paid',
 sum(case when Cash_Type_VC = 'OA' and Cash_Category_VC = 'OA_Int'
and Year_SI = 2007 and GL_ID = 2002
 then Journal_T.Amount_NU else 0 end)

from Cash_T join Journal_T on
Cash_T.Doc_No_VC = Journal_T.Doc_No_VC

union all

select 'Income taxes paid',
 sum(case when Cash_Type_VC = 'OA' and Cash_Category_VC = 'OA_Tax'
and Year_SI = 2007 and GL_ID = 2002
 then Journal_T.Amount_NU else 0 end)

from Cash_T join Journal_T on
Cash_T.Doc_No_VC = Journal_T.Doc_No_VC

union all

select 'Net Cash Outflow from Operating Activities :' ,
 sum(Journal_T.Amount_NU)

from Cash_T join Journal_T on
Cash_T.Doc_No_VC = Journal_T.Doc_No_VC where
Cash_Type_VC      =      'OA'      and      Cash_Category_VC      in
('OA_Deb','OA_Sup','OA_Int','OA_Tax') and Year_SI = 2007 and
```

```
GL_ID = 2002
having sum(Journal_T.Amount_NU) < 0

union all

select 'Net Cash Inflow from Operating Activities :' ,
 sum(Journal_T.Amount_NU)

from Cash_T join Journal_T on
Cash_T.Doc_No_VC = Journal_T.Doc_No_VC where
Cash_Type_VC        =        'OA'        and        Cash_Category_VC        in
('OA_Deb','OA_Sup','OA_Int','OA_Tax') and Year_SI = 2007 and
GL_ID = 2002
having sum(Journal_T.Amount_NU) > 0

union all

select 'Cash from Investing Activities :',
 sum(case when Cash_Type_VC = 'aaa' then Journal_T.Amount_NU else
 0 end) as [$]

from Cash_T join Journal_T on
Cash_T.Doc_No_VC = Journal_T.Doc_No_VC

union all

select 'Purchase of PPE',
 sum(case when Cash_Type_VC = 'IA' and Cash_Category_VC = 'IA_Pur'
and Year_SI = 2007 and GL_ID = 2002
 then Journal_T.Amount_NU else 0 end)

from Cash_T join Journal_T on
Cash_T.Doc_No_VC = Journal_T.Doc_No_VC

union all

select 'Proceeds from disposal of PPE',
 sum(case when Cash_Type_VC = 'IA' and Cash_Category_VC = 'IA_Pro'
and Year_SI = 2007 and GL_ID = 2002
 then Journal_T.Amount_NU else 0 end)

from Cash_T join Journal_T on
Cash_T.Doc_No_VC = Journal_T.Doc_No_VC

union all

select 'Interest received',
 sum(case when Cash_Type_VC = 'IA' and Cash_Category_VC = 'IA_Int'
and Year_SI = 2007 and GL_ID = 2002
 then Journal_T.Amount_NU else 0 end)

from Cash_T join Journal_T on
```

```sql
Cash_T.Doc_No_VC = Journal_T.Doc_No_VC

union all
select 'Net Cash Outflow from Investing Activities :' ,
 sum(Journal_T.Amount_NU)

from Cash_T join Journal_T on
Cash_T.Doc_No_VC = Journal_T.Doc_No_VC where
Cash_Type_VC        =        'IA'        and        Cash_Category_VC        in
('IA_Int','IA_Pur','IA_Pro') and Year_SI = 2007 and GL_ID = 2002
having sum(Journal_T.Amount_NU) < 0

union all

select 'Net Cash Inflow from Investing Activities :' ,
 sum(Journal_T.Amount_NU)

from Cash_T join Journal_T on
Cash_T.Doc_No_VC = Journal_T.Doc_No_VC where
Cash_Type_VC        =        'IA'        and        Cash_Category_VC        in
('IA_Int','IA_Pur','IA_Pro') and Year_SI = 2007 and GL_ID = 2002
having sum(Journal_T.Amount_NU) > 0

union all

select 'Cash from Financing Activities :',
 sum(case when Cash_Type_VC = 'aaa' then Journal_T.Amount_NU else
 0 end) as [$]

from Cash_T join Journal_T on
Cash_T.Doc_No_VC = Journal_T.Doc_No_VC

union all

select 'Proceeds from issue of share capital',
 sum(case when Cash_Type_VC = 'FA' and Cash_Category_VC = 'FA_Cap'
and Year_SI = 2007 and GL_ID = 2002
 then Journal_T.Amount_NU else 0 end)

from Cash_T join Journal_T on
Cash_T.Doc_No_VC = Journal_T.Doc_No_VC

union all

select 'Net Cash Outflow from Financing Activities :' ,
 sum(Journal_T.Amount_NU)

from Cash_T join Journal_T on
Cash_T.Doc_No_VC = Journal_T.Doc_No_VC where
Cash_Type_VC = 'FA' and Cash_Category_VC in ('FA_Cap') and Year_SI =
2007 and GL_ID = 2002
having sum(Journal_T.Amount_NU) < 0
```

```
union all

select 'Net Cash Inflow from Financing Activities :' ,
 sum(Journal_T.Amount_NU)

from Cash_T join Journal_T on
Cash_T.Doc_No_VC = Journal_T.Doc_No_VC where
Cash_Type_VC = 'FA' and Cash_Category_VC in ('FA_Cap') and Year_SI =
2007 and GL_ID = 2002

having sum(Journal_T.Amount_NU) > 0

union all

select 'Net Decrease in Cash & Cash equivalent :' ,
 sum(Journal_T.Amount_NU)

from Cash_T join Journal_T on
Cash_T.Doc_No_VC = Journal_T.Doc_No_VC where
Cash_Type_VC in ('OA','IA','FA') and Year_SI = 2007 and GL_ID = 2002
having sum(Journal_T.Amount_NU) < 0

union all

select 'Net Increase in Cash & Cash equivalent :' ,
 sum(Journal_T.Amount_NU)

from Cash_T join Journal_T on
Cash_T.Doc_No_VC = Journal_T.Doc_No_VC where
Cash_Type_VC in ('OA','IA','FA') and Year_SI = 2007 and GL_ID = 2002
having sum(Journal_T.Amount_NU) > 0
```

Now, test your query, by clicking on the parse query button to check for any syntax error, if your syntax is working, you would see the message "The command(s) completed successfully." If not, go through the code above again, and run the parse query until your syntax is working properly. Then, execute the query, by clicking on the execute query button, and you would see the following output appearing on your result pane.

	Cash Flow Statement	$
1	Cash from Operating Activities :	0
2	Cash receipt from Customer	4000
3	Cash paid to Supplier	0
4	Cash generated from Operations	4000
5	Interest paid	-745
6	Income taxes paid	-600
7	Net Cash Inflow from Operating Activities :	2655
8	Cash from Investing Activities :	0
9	Purchase of PPE	-1710
10	Proceeds from disposal of PPE	0
11	Interest received	250
12	Net Cash Outflow from Investing Activities :	-1460
13	Cash from Financing Activities :	0
14	Proceeds from issue of share capital	2000
15	Net Cash Inflow from Financing Activities :	2000
16	Net Increase in Cash & Cash equivalent :	3195

As we can see from the above report, MaxCorp's cash flow can be better analyzed, when its cash flow is broken down into three categories that we have mentioned earlier.

How It Works – Select Query for Cash Flow Summary Statement Report

Let us analyze the function of our select query. We have two columns in our cash flow statement, to place our records. We want to place the header name 'Cash from Operating Activities :' on our first column, so we select this on our first selection, next we do not want to place anything beside the header, so we create a fictitious selection of a non-existence record, in this way, our selection would always return the output as 0.

On our next block of query, we want to pull records from the bank account code, 2002, that are categorized as 'OA_Deb' and with the cash type 'OA'. We sum up the amount, and place it on our second column, beside our static text, 'Cash receipt from Customer'. We know that the cash receipt amount is derived from the Journal Table, the cash type and category are from the Cash Table, so we combine these two tables in our query.

```
select 'Cash from Operating Activities :' as [Cash Flow Statement],
  sum(case when Cash_Type_VC = 'aaa' then Journal_T.Amount_NU else
  0 end) as [$]
```

```
from Cash_T join Journal_T on
Cash_T.Doc_No_VC = Journal_T.Doc_No_VC

union all

select 'Cash receipt from Customer',
 sum(case when Cash_Type_VC = 'OA' and Cash_Category_VC = 'OA_Deb'
and Year_SI = 2007 and GL_ID = 2002
 then Journal_T.Amount_NU else 0 end)

from Cash_T join Journal_T on
Cash_T.Doc_No_VC = Journal_T.Doc_No_VC
```

Next, we want to pull payment records from the Journal Table, so we specify the bank account code of 2002, the cash type of 'OA' and cash category of 'OA_Sup' from the Cash Table, and place the amount on our second column, beside the static text, 'Cash paid to Supplier'. We then join the Cash Table and Journals Table together using inner join.

```
union all

select 'Cash paid to Supplier',
 sum(case when Cash_Type_VC = 'OA' and Cash_Category_VC = 'OA_Sup'
and Year_SI = 2007 and GL_ID = 2002
 then Journal_T.Amount_NU else 0 end)

from Cash_T join Journal_T on
Cash_T.Doc_No_VC = Journal_T.Doc_No_VC
```

If you look through the rest of the queries, you will be able to identify the similar function of each block of query. Let us jump to our last two block of query as follows.

Our first block of query, would determine the net amount of all the three categories added together, and place them as Net Decrease in Cash, if the net amount is lesser than 0. If the net amount is greater than 0, we would then, place the amount as Net Increase in Cash, as specified in our second block of query. This time, we specify all three categories together in our filtering condition. We join the Cash Table and the Journals Table together via its common fields.

```
select 'Net Decrease in Cash & Cash equivalent :' ,
 sum(Journal_T.Amount_NU)

from Cash_T join Journal_T on
Cash_T.Doc_No_VC = Journal_T.Doc_No_VC where
Cash_Type_VC in ('OA','IA','FA') and Year_SI = 2007 and GL_ID = 2002
having sum(Journal_T.Amount_NU) < 0
```

```
union all

select 'Net Increase in Cash & Cash equivalent :' ,
 sum(Journal_T.Amount_NU)

from Cash_T join Journal_T on
Cash_T.Doc_No_VC = Journal_T.Doc_No_VC where
Cash_Type_VC in ('OA','IA','FA') and Year_SI = 2007 and GL_ID = 2002
having sum(Journal_T.Amount_NU) > 0
```

3) Using SQL to produce Cash Flow Periodic Statement

This report is basically the same as the Cash Flow Summary, except, it is broken down in periods, with greater level of details.

Let us enter the following select query as follows

```
select 'Cash from Operating Activities :' as [Cash Flow],
 sum(case when Cash_Type_VC = 'aaa' then Journal_T.Amount_NU else
 0 end) as [Period 01],
 sum(case when Cash_Type_VC = 'aaa' then Journal_T.Amount_NU else
 0 end) as [Period 02],
 sum(case when Cash_Type_VC = 'aaa' then Journal_T.Amount_NU else
 0 end) as [Period 03],
 sum(case when Cash_Type_VC = 'aaa' then Journal_T.Amount_NU else
 0 end) as [Period 04],
 sum(case when Cash_Type_VC = 'aaa' then Journal_T.Amount_NU else
 0 end) as [Period 05],
 sum(case when Cash_Type_VC = 'aaa' then Journal_T.Amount_NU else
 0 end) as [Period 06],

sum(case when Cash_Type_VC = 'aaa' then Journal_T.Amount_NU else 0
end) as [Period 07],
 sum(case when Cash_Type_VC = 'aaa' then Journal_T.Amount_NU else
 0 end) as [Period 08],
 sum(case when Cash_Type_VC = 'aaa' then Journal_T.Amount_NU else
 0 end) as [Period 09],
 sum(case when Cash_Type_VC = 'aaa' then Journal_T.Amount_NU else
 0 end) as [Period 10],
 sum(case when Cash_Type_VC = 'aaa' then Journal_T.Amount_NU else
 0 end) as [Period 11],
 sum(case when Cash_Type_VC = 'aaa' then Journal_T.Amount_NU else
 0 end) as [Period 12],
 sum(case when Cash_Type_VC = 'aaa' then Journal_T.Amount_NU else
 0 end) as [YTD]

from Cash_T join Journal_T on
Cash_T.Doc_No_VC = Journal_T.Doc_No_VC

union all
```

```sql
select Descrip_VC,
 case when Cash_Type_VC = 'OA' and Cash_Category_VC = 'OA_Deb' and
 Period_TI = 1 and Year_SI = 2007 then Journal_T.Amount_NU else 0
end,
 case when Cash_Type_VC = 'OA' and Cash_Category_VC = 'OA_Deb' and
 Period_TI = 2 and Year_SI = 2007 then Journal_T.Amount_NU else 0
end,
 case when Cash_Type_VC = 'OA' and Cash_Category_VC = 'OA_Deb' and
 Period_TI = 3 and Year_SI = 2007 then Journal_T.Amount_NU else 0
end,
 case when Cash_Type_VC = 'OA' and Cash_Category_VC = 'OA_Deb' and
 Period_TI = 4 and Year_SI = 2007 then Journal_T.Amount_NU else 0
end,
 case when Cash_Type_VC = 'OA' and Cash_Category_VC = 'OA_Deb' and
 Period_TI = 5 and Year_SI = 2007 then Journal_T.Amount_NU else 0
end,
 case when Cash_Type_VC = 'OA' and Cash_Category_VC = 'OA_Deb' and
 Period_TI = 6 and Year_SI = 2007 then Journal_T.Amount_NU else 0
end,
 case when Cash_Type_VC = 'OA' and Cash_Category_VC = 'OA_Deb' and
 Period_TI = 7 and Year_SI = 2007 then Journal_T.Amount_NU else 0
end,
 case when Cash_Type_VC = 'OA' and Cash_Category_VC = 'OA_Deb' and
 Period_TI = 8 and Year_SI = 2007 then Journal_T.Amount_NU else 0
end,
 case when Cash_Type_VC = 'OA' and Cash_Category_VC = 'OA_Deb' and
 Period_TI = 9 and Year_SI = 2007 then Journal_T.Amount_NU else 0
end,
 case when Cash_Type_VC = 'OA' and Cash_Category_VC = 'OA_Deb' and
 Period_TI = 10 and Year_SI = 2007 then Journal_T.Amount_NU else 0
end,
 case when Cash_Type_VC = 'OA' and Cash_Category_VC = 'OA_Deb' and
 Period_TI = 11 and Year_SI = 2007 then Journal_T.Amount_NU else 0
end,
 case when Cash_Type_VC = 'OA' and Cash_Category_VC = 'OA_Deb' and
 Period_TI = 12 and Year_SI = 2007 then Journal_T.Amount_NU else 0
end,
 case when Cash_Type_VC = 'OA' and Cash_Category_VC = 'OA_Deb' and
 Year_SI = 2007 then Journal_T.Amount_NU else 0 end

from Cash_T join Journal_T on
Cash_T.Doc_No_VC = Journal_T.Doc_No_VC
where Cash_Type_VC = 'OA' and Cash_Category_VC = 'OA_Deb' and
Year_SI = 2007 and GL_ID = 2002

union all

select Descrip_VC,
 case when Cash_Type_VC = 'OA' and Cash_Category_VC = 'OA_Sup' and
 Period_TI = 1 and Year_SI = 2007 then Journal_T.Amount_NU else 0
end,
```

```sql
 case when Cash_Type_VC = 'OA' and Cash_Category_VC = 'OA_Sup' and
 Period_TI = 2 and Year_SI = 2007 then Journal_T.Amount_NU else 0
end,
 case when Cash_Type_VC = 'OA' and Cash_Category_VC = 'OA_Sup' and
 Period_TI = 3 and Year_SI = 2007 then Journal_T.Amount_NU else 0
end,
 case when Cash_Type_VC = 'OA' and Cash_Category_VC = 'OA_Sup' and
 Period_TI = 4 and Year_SI = 2007 then Journal_T.Amount_NU else 0
end,
 case when Cash_Type_VC = 'OA' and Cash_Category_VC = 'OA_Sup' and
 Period_TI = 5 and Year_SI = 2007 then Journal_T.Amount_NU else 0
end,
 case when Cash_Type_VC = 'OA' and Cash_Category_VC = 'OA_Sup' and
 Period_TI = 6 and Year_SI = 2007 then Journal_T.Amount_NU else 0
end,
 case when Cash_Type_VC = 'OA' and Cash_Category_VC = 'OA_Sup' and
 Period_TI = 7 and Year_SI = 2007 then Journal_T.Amount_NU else 0
end,
 case when Cash_Type_VC = 'OA' and Cash_Category_VC = 'OA_Sup' and
 Period_TI = 8 and Year_SI = 2007 then Journal_T.Amount_NU else 0
end,
 case when Cash_Type_VC = 'OA' and Cash_Category_VC = 'OA_Sup' and
 Period_TI = 9 and Year_SI = 2007 then Journal_T.Amount_NU else 0
end,
 case when Cash_Type_VC = 'OA' and Cash_Category_VC = 'OA_Sup' and
 Period_TI = 10 and Year_SI = 2007 then Journal_T.Amount_NU else 0
end,
 case when Cash_Type_VC = 'OA' and Cash_Category_VC = 'OA_Sup' and
 Period_TI = 11 and Year_SI = 2007 then Journal_T.Amount_NU else 0
end,
 case when Cash_Type_VC = 'OA' and Cash_Category_VC = 'OA_Sup' and
 Period_TI = 12 and Year_SI = 2007 then Journal_T.Amount_NU else 0
end,
 case when Cash_Type_VC = 'OA' and Cash_Category_VC = 'OA_Sup' and
 Year_SI = 2007 then Journal_T.Amount_NU else 0 end

from Cash_T join Journal_T on
Cash_T.Doc_No_VC = Journal_T.Doc_No_VC
where  Cash_Type_VC  =  'OA'  and  Cash_Category_VC  =  'OA_Sup'  and
Year_SI = 2007 and GL_ID = 2002

union all

select 'Cash generated from Operations',
 sum(case when Cash_Type_VC = 'OA' and Cash_Category_VC in
 ('OA_Deb','OA_Sup')and Period_TI = 1 and Year_SI = 2007 and
 GL_ID = 2002 then Journal_T.Amount_NU else 0 end),
 sum(case when Cash_Type_VC = 'OA' and Cash_Category_VC in
 ('OA_Deb','OA_Sup')and Period_TI = 2 and Year_SI = 2007 and
 GL_ID = 2002 then Journal_T.Amount_NU else 0 end),
 sum(case when Cash_Type_VC = 'OA' and Cash_Category_VC in
 ('OA_Deb','OA_Sup')and Period_TI = 3 and Year_SI = 2007 and
```

```
 GL_ID = 2002 then Journal_T.Amount_NU else 0 end),
 sum(case when Cash_Type_VC = 'OA' and Cash_Category_VC in
 ('OA_Deb','OA_Sup')and Period_TI = 4 and Year_SI = 2007 and
 GL_ID = 2002 then Journal_T.Amount_NU else 0 end),
 sum(case when Cash_Type_VC = 'OA' and Cash_Category_VC in
 ('OA_Deb','OA_Sup')and Period_TI = 5 and Year_SI = 2007 and
 GL_ID = 2002 then Journal_T.Amount_NU else 0 end),
 sum(case when Cash_Type_VC = 'OA' and Cash_Category_VC in
 ('OA_Deb','OA_Sup')and Period_TI = 6 and Year_SI = 2007 and
 GL_ID = 2002 then Journal_T.Amount_NU else 0 end),


 sum(case when Cash_Type_VC = 'OA' and Cash_Category_VC in
 ('OA_Deb','OA_Sup')and Period_TI = 7 and Year_SI = 2007 and
 GL_ID = 2002 then Journal_T.Amount_NU else 0 end),
 sum(case when Cash_Type_VC = 'OA' and Cash_Category_VC in
 ('OA_Deb','OA_Sup')and Period_TI = 8 and Year_SI = 2007 and
 GL_ID = 2002 then Journal_T.Amount_NU else 0 end),
 sum(case when Cash_Type_VC = 'OA' and Cash_Category_VC in
 ('OA_Deb','OA_Sup')and Period_TI = 9 and Year_SI = 2007 and
 GL_ID = 2002 then Journal_T.Amount_NU else 0 end),
 sum(case when Cash_Type_VC = 'OA' and Cash_Category_VC in
 ('OA_Deb','OA_Sup')and Period_TI = 10 and Year_SI = 2007 and
 GL_ID = 2002 then Journal_T.Amount_NU else 0 end),
 sum(case when Cash_Type_VC = 'OA' and Cash_Category_VC in
 ('OA_Deb','OA_Sup')and Period_TI = 11 and Year_SI = 2007 and
 GL_ID = 2002 then Journal_T.Amount_NU else 0 end),
 sum(case when Cash_Type_VC = 'OA' and Cash_Category_VC in
 ('OA_Deb','OA_Sup')and Period_TI = 12 and Year_SI = 2007 and
 GL_ID = 2002 then Journal_T.Amount_NU else 0 end),
 sum(case when Cash_Type_VC = 'OA' and Cash_Category_VC in
 ('OA_Deb','OA_Sup')and Year_SI = 2007 and GL_ID = 2002
  then Journal_T.Amount_NU else 0 end)

from Cash_T join Journal_T on
Cash_T.Doc_No_VC = Journal_T.Doc_No_VC

union all

select Descrip_VC,
 case when Cash_Type_VC = 'OA' and Cash_Category_VC = 'OA_Int' and
 Period_TI = 1 and Year_SI = 2007 then Journal_T.Amount_NU else 0
end,
 case when Cash_Type_VC = 'OA' and Cash_Category_VC = 'OA_Int' and
 Period_TI = 2 and Year_SI = 2007 then Journal_T.Amount_NU else 0
end,
 case when Cash_Type_VC = 'OA' and Cash_Category_VC = 'OA_Int' and
 Period_TI = 3 and Year_SI = 2007 then Journal_T.Amount_NU else 0
end,
 case when Cash_Type_VC = 'OA' and Cash_Category_VC = 'OA_Int' and
 Period_TI = 4 and Year_SI = 2007 then Journal_T.Amount_NU else 0
end,
```

```sql
 case when Cash_Type_VC = 'OA' and Cash_Category_VC = 'OA_Int' and
 Period_TI = 5 and Year_SI = 2007 then Journal_T.Amount_NU else 0
end,
 case when Cash_Type_VC = 'OA' and Cash_Category_VC = 'OA_Int' and
 Period_TI = 6 and Year_SI = 2007 then Journal_T.Amount_NU else 0
end,
 case when Cash_Type_VC = 'OA' and Cash_Category_VC = 'OA_Int' and
 Period_TI = 7 and Year_SI = 2007 then Journal_T.Amount_NU else 0
end,
 case when Cash_Type_VC = 'OA' and Cash_Category_VC = 'OA_Int' and
 Period_TI = 8 and Year_SI = 2007 then Journal_T.Amount_NU else 0
end,
 case when Cash_Type_VC = 'OA' and Cash_Category_VC = 'OA_Int' and
 Period_TI = 9 and Year_SI = 2007 then Journal_T.Amount_NU else 0
end,
 case when Cash_Type_VC = 'OA' and Cash_Category_VC = 'OA_Int' and
 Period_TI = 10 and Year_SI = 2007 then Journal_T.Amount_NU else 0
end,
 case when Cash_Type_VC = 'OA' and Cash_Category_VC = 'OA_Int' and
 Period_TI = 11 and Year_SI = 2007 then Journal_T.Amount_NU else 0
end,
 case when Cash_Type_VC = 'OA' and Cash_Category_VC = 'OA_Int' and
 Period_TI = 12 and Year_SI = 2007 then Journal_T.Amount_NU else 0
end,
 case when Cash_Type_VC = 'OA' and Cash_Category_VC = 'OA_Int' and
 Year_SI = 2007 then Journal_T.Amount_NU else 0 end

from Cash_T join Journal_T on
Cash_T.Doc_No_VC = Journal_T.Doc_No_VC
where Cash_Type_VC = 'OA' and Cash_Category_VC = 'OA_Int' and
Year_SI = 2007 and GL_ID = 2002

union all

select Descrip_VC,
 case when Cash_Type_VC = 'OA' and Cash_Category_VC = 'OA_Tax' and
 Period_TI = 1 and Year_SI = 2007 then Journal_T.Amount_NU else 0
end,
 case when Cash_Type_VC = 'OA' and Cash_Category_VC = 'OA_Tax' and
 Period_TI = 2 and Year_SI = 2007 then Journal_T.Amount_NU else 0
end,
 case when Cash_Type_VC = 'OA' and Cash_Category_VC = 'OA_Tax' and
 Period_TI = 3 and Year_SI = 2007 then Journal_T.Amount_NU else 0
end,
 case when Cash_Type_VC = 'OA' and Cash_Category_VC = 'OA_Tax' and
 Period_TI = 4 and Year_SI = 2007 then Journal_T.Amount_NU else 0
end,
 case when Cash_Type_VC = 'OA' and Cash_Category_VC = 'OA_Tax' and
 Period_TI = 5 and Year_SI = 2007 then Journal_T.Amount_NU else 0
end,
 case when Cash_Type_VC = 'OA' and Cash_Category_VC = 'OA_Tax' and
```

```sql
 Period_TI = 6 and Year_SI = 2007 then Journal_T.Amount_NU else 0
end,
 case when Cash_Type_VC = 'OA' and Cash_Category_VC = 'OA_Tax' and
 Period_TI = 7 and Year_SI = 2007 then Journal_T.Amount_NU else 0
end,
 case when Cash_Type_VC = 'OA' and Cash_Category_VC = 'OA_Tax' and
 Period_TI = 8 and Year_SI = 2007 then Journal_T.Amount_NU else 0
end,
 case when Cash_Type_VC = 'OA' and Cash_Category_VC = 'OA_Tax' and
 Period_TI = 9 and Year_SI = 2007 then Journal_T.Amount_NU else 0
end,
 case when Cash_Type_VC = 'OA' and Cash_Category_VC = 'OA_Tax' and
 Period_TI = 10 and Year_SI = 2007 then Journal_T.Amount_NU else 0
end,
 case when Cash_Type_VC = 'OA' and Cash_Category_VC = 'OA_Tax' and
 Period_TI = 11 and Year_SI = 2007 then Journal_T.Amount_NU else 0
end,
 case when Cash_Type_VC = 'OA' and Cash_Category_VC = 'OA_Tax' and
 Period_TI = 12 and Year_SI = 2007 then Journal_T.Amount_NU else 0
end,
 case when Cash_Type_VC = 'OA' and Cash_Category_VC = 'OA_Tax' and
 Year_SI = 2007 then Journal_T.Amount_NU else 0 end

from Cash_T join Journal_T on
Cash_T.Doc_No_VC = Journal_T.Doc_No_VC
where  Cash_Type_VC  =  'OA'  and  Cash_Category_VC  =  'OA_Tax'  and
Year_SI = 2007 and GL_ID = 2002

union all

select 'Net Cash Flow from Operating Activities',
 sum(case when Cash_Type_VC = 'OA' and Cash_Category_VC in
 ('OA_Deb','OA_Sup','OA_Int','OA_Tax')and Period_TI = 1 and
 Year_SI = 2007 and GL_ID = 2002 then Journal_T.Amount_NU else 0
end),
 sum(case when Cash_Type_VC = 'OA' and Cash_Category_VC in
 ('OA_Deb','OA_Sup','OA_Int','OA_Tax')and Period_TI = 2 and
 Year_SI = 2007 and GL_ID = 2002 then Journal_T.Amount_NU else 0
end),
 sum(case when Cash_Type_VC = 'OA' and Cash_Category_VC in
 ('OA_Deb','OA_Sup','OA_Int','OA_Tax')and Period_TI = 3 and
 Year_SI = 2007 and GL_ID = 2002 then Journal_T.Amount_NU else 0
end),
 sum(case when Cash_Type_VC = 'OA' and Cash_Category_VC in
 ('OA_Deb','OA_Sup','OA_Int','OA_Tax')and Period_TI = 4 and
 Year_SI = 2007 and GL_ID = 2002 then Journal_T.Amount_NU else 0
end),

sum(case   when   Cash_Type_VC   =   'OA'   and   Cash_Category_VC   in
('OA_Deb','OA_Sup','OA_Int','OA_Tax')and Period_TI = 5 and
Year_SI = 2007 and GL_ID = 2002 then Journal_T.Amount_NU else 0
end),
```

```sql
sum(case    when    Cash_Type_VC    =    'OA'    and    Cash_Category_VC    in
('OA_Deb','OA_Sup','OA_Int','OA_Tax')and Period_TI = 6 and
Year_SI = 2007 and GL_ID = 2002 then Journal_T.Amount_NU else 0
end),
sum(case    when    Cash_Type_VC    =    'OA'    and    Cash_Category_VC    in
('OA_Deb','OA_Sup','OA_Int','OA_Tax')and Period_TI = 7 and
Year_SI = 2007 and GL_ID = 2002 then Journal_T.Amount_NU else 0
end),
sum(case    when    Cash_Type_VC    =    'OA'    and    Cash_Category_VC    in
('OA_Deb','OA_Sup','OA_Int','OA_Tax')and Period_TI = 8 and
Year_SI = 2007 and GL_ID = 2002 then Journal_T.Amount_NU else 0
end),
sum(case    when    Cash_Type_VC    =    'OA'    and    Cash_Category_VC    in
('OA_Deb','OA_Sup','OA_Int','OA_Tax')and Period_TI = 9 and
Year_SI = 2007 and GL_ID = 2002 then Journal_T.Amount_NU else 0
end),
sum(case    when    Cash_Type_VC    =    'OA'    and    Cash_Category_VC    in
('OA_Deb','OA_Sup','OA_Int','OA_Tax')and Period_TI = 10 and
Year_SI = 2007 and GL_ID = 2002 then Journal_T.Amount_NU else 0
end),
sum(case    when    Cash_Type_VC    =    'OA'    and    Cash_Category_VC    in
('OA_Deb','OA_Sup','OA_Int','OA_Tax')and Period_TI = 11 and
Year_SI = 2007 and GL_ID = 2002 then Journal_T.Amount_NU else 0
end),
sum(case    when    Cash_Type_VC    =    'OA'    and    Cash_Category_VC    in
('OA_Deb','OA_Sup','OA_Int','OA_Tax')and Period_TI = 12 and
Year_SI = 2007 and GL_ID = 2002 then Journal_T.Amount_NU else 0
end),
sum(case    when    Cash_Type_VC    =    'OA'    and    Cash_Category_VC    in
('OA_Deb','OA_Sup','OA_Int','OA_Tax')and Year_SI = 2007 and
GL_ID = 2002 then Journal_T.Amount_NU else 0 end)

from Cash_T join Journal_T on
Cash_T.Doc_No_VC = Journal_T.Doc_No_VC

union all

select 'Cash from Investing Activities :' as [Cash Flow],
 sum(case when Cash_Type_VC = 'aaa' then
 Amount_NU else 0 end) as [Period 01],
 sum(case when Cash_Type_VC = 'aaa' then
 Amount_NU else 0 end) as [Period 02],
 sum(case when Cash_Type_VC = 'aaa' then
 Amount_NU else 0 end) as [Period 03],
 sum(case when Cash_Type_VC = 'aaa' then
 Amount_NU else 0 end) as [Period 04],
 sum(case when Cash_Type_VC = 'aaa' then
 Amount_NU else 0 end) as [Period 05],
 sum(case when Cash_Type_VC = 'aaa' then
 Amount_NU else 0 end) as [Period 06],
 sum(case when Cash_Type_VC = 'aaa' then
 Amount_NU else 0 end) as [Period 07],
```

```
  sum(case when Cash_Type_VC = 'aaa' then
  Amount_NU else 0 end) as [Period 08],
  sum(case when Cash_Type_VC = 'aaa' then
  Amount_NU else 0 end) as [Period 09],
  sum(case when Cash_Type_VC = 'aaa' then
  Amount_NU else 0 end) as [Period 10],

  sum(case when Cash_Type_VC = 'aaa' then
  Amount_NU else 0 end) as [Period 11],
  sum(case when Cash_Type_VC = 'aaa' then
  Amount_NU else 0 end) as [Period 12],
  sum(case when Cash_Type_VC = 'aaa' then
  Amount_NU else 0 end) as [YTD]

from Cash_T join Journal_T on
Cash_T.Doc_No_VC = Journal_T.Doc_No_VC

union all

select Descrip_VC,
  case when Cash_Type_VC = 'IA' and Cash_Category_VC = 'IA_Pur' and
  Period_TI = 1 and Year_SI = 2007 then Journal_T.Amount_NU else 0
end,
  case when Cash_Type_VC = 'IA' and Cash_Category_VC = 'IA_Pur' and
  Period_TI = 2 and Year_SI = 2007 then Journal_T.Amount_NU else 0
end,
  case when Cash_Type_VC = 'IA' and Cash_Category_VC = 'IA_Pur' and
  Period_TI = 3 and Year_SI = 2007 then Journal_T.Amount_NU else 0
end,
  case when Cash_Type_VC = 'IA' and Cash_Category_VC = 'IA_Pur' and
  Period_TI = 4 and Year_SI = 2007 then Journal_T.Amount_NU else 0
end,
  case when Cash_Type_VC = 'IA' and Cash_Category_VC = 'IA_Pur' and
  Period_TI = 5 and Year_SI = 2007 then Journal_T.Amount_NU else 0
end,
  case when Cash_Type_VC = 'IA' and Cash_Category_VC = 'IA_Pur' and
  Period_TI = 6 and Year_SI = 2007 then Journal_T.Amount_NU else 0
end,
  case when Cash_Type_VC = 'IA' and Cash_Category_VC = 'IA_Pur' and
  Period_TI = 7 and Year_SI = 2007 then Journal_T.Amount_NU else 0
end,
  case when Cash_Type_VC = 'IA' and Cash_Category_VC = 'IA_Pur' and
  Period_TI = 8 and Year_SI = 2007 then Journal_T.Amount_NU else 0
end,
  case when Cash_Type_VC = 'IA' and Cash_Category_VC = 'IA_Pur' and
  Period_TI = 9 and Year_SI = 2007 then Journal_T.Amount_NU else 0
end,
  case when Cash_Type_VC = 'IA' and Cash_Category_VC = 'IA_Pur' and
  Period_TI = 10 and Year_SI = 2007 then Journal_T.Amount_NU else 0
end,
  case when Cash_Type_VC = 'IA' and Cash_Category_VC = 'IA_Pur' and
```

```sql
 Period_TI = 11 and Year_SI = 2007 then Journal_T.Amount_NU else 0
end,
 case when Cash_Type_VC = 'IA' and Cash_Category_VC = 'IA_Pur' and
 Period_TI = 12 and Year_SI = 2007 then Journal_T.Amount_NU else 0
end,
 case when Cash_Type_VC = 'IA' and Cash_Category_VC = 'IA_Pur' and
 Year_SI = 2007 then Journal_T.Amount_NU else 0 end

from Cash_T join Journal_T on
Cash_T.Doc_No_VC = Journal_T.Doc_No_VC
where  Cash_Type_VC = 'IA' and  Cash_Category_VC = 'IA_Pur'  and
Year_SI = 2007 and GL_ID = 2002

union all

select Descrip_VC,
 case when Cash_Type_VC = 'IA' and Cash_Category_VC = 'IA_Pro' and
 Period_TI = 1 and Year_SI = 2007 then Journal_T.Amount_NU else 0
end,
 case when Cash_Type_VC = 'IA' and Cash_Category_VC = 'IA_Pro' and
 Period_TI = 2 and Year_SI = 2007 then Journal_T.Amount_NU else 0
end,
 case when Cash_Type_VC = 'IA' and Cash_Category_VC = 'IA_Pro' and
 Period_TI = 3 and Year_SI = 2007 then Journal_T.Amount_NU else 0
end,
 case when Cash_Type_VC = 'IA' and Cash_Category_VC = 'IA_Pro' and
 Period_TI = 4 and Year_SI = 2007 then Journal_T.Amount_NU else 0
end,

 case when Cash_Type_VC = 'IA' and Cash_Category_VC = 'IA_Pro' and
 Period_TI = 5 and Year_SI = 2007 then Journal_T.Amount_NU else 0
end,
 case when Cash_Type_VC = 'IA' and Cash_Category_VC = 'IA_Pro' and
 Period_TI = 6 and Year_SI = 2007 then Journal_T.Amount_NU else 0
end,
 case when Cash_Type_VC = 'IA' and Cash_Category_VC = 'IA_Pro' and
 Period_TI = 7 and Year_SI = 2007 then Journal_T.Amount_NU else 0
end,
 case when Cash_Type_VC = 'IA' and Cash_Category_VC = 'IA_Pro' and
 Period_TI = 8 and Year_SI = 2007 then Journal_T.Amount_NU else 0
end,
 case when Cash_Type_VC = 'IA' and Cash_Category_VC = 'IA_Pro' and
 Period_TI = 9 and Year_SI = 2007 then Journal_T.Amount_NU else 0
end,
 case when Cash_Type_VC = 'IA' and Cash_Category_VC = 'IA_Pro' and
 Period_TI = 10 and Year_SI = 2007 then Journal_T.Amount_NU else 0
end,
 case when Cash_Type_VC = 'IA' and Cash_Category_VC = 'IA_Pro' and
 Period_TI = 11 and Year_SI = 2007 then Journal_T.Amount_NU else 0
end,
 case when Cash_Type_VC = 'IA' and Cash_Category_VC = 'IA_Pro' and
```

```
 Period_TI = 12 and Year_SI = 2007 then Journal_T.Amount_NU else 0
end,
 case when Cash_Type_VC = 'IA' and Cash_Category_VC = 'IA_Pro' and
 Year_SI = 2007 then Journal_T.Amount_NU else 0 end

from Cash_T join Journal_T on
Cash_T.Doc_No_VC = Journal_T.Doc_No_VC
where  Cash_Type_VC  =  'IA'  and  Cash_Category_VC  =  'IA_Pro'  and
Year_SI = 2007 and GL_ID = 2002

union all

select Descrip_VC,
 case when Cash_Type_VC = 'IA' and Cash_Category_VC = 'IA_Int' and
 Period_TI = 1 and Year_SI = 2007 then Journal_T.Amount_NU else 0
end,
 case when Cash_Type_VC = 'IA' and Cash_Category_VC = 'IA_Int' and
 Period_TI = 2 and Year_SI = 2007 then Journal_T.Amount_NU else 0
end,
 case when Cash_Type_VC = 'IA' and Cash_Category_VC = 'IA_Int' and
 Period_TI = 3 and Year_SI = 2007 then Journal_T.Amount_NU else 0
end,
 case when Cash_Type_VC = 'IA' and Cash_Category_VC = 'IA_Int' and
 Period_TI = 4 and Year_SI = 2007 then Journal_T.Amount_NU else 0
end,
 case when Cash_Type_VC = 'IA' and Cash_Category_VC = 'IA_Int' and
 Period_TI = 5 and Year_SI = 2007 then Journal_T.Amount_NU else 0
end,
 case when Cash_Type_VC = 'IA' and Cash_Category_VC = 'IA_Int' and
 Period_TI = 6 and Year_SI = 2007 then Journal_T.Amount_NU else 0
end,
 case when Cash_Type_VC = 'IA' and Cash_Category_VC = 'IA_Int' and
 Period_TI = 7 and Year_SI = 2007 then Journal_T.Amount_NU else 0
end,
 case when Cash_Type_VC = 'IA' and Cash_Category_VC = 'IA_Int' and
 Period_TI = 8 and Year_SI = 2007 then Journal_T.Amount_NU else 0
end,
 case when Cash_Type_VC = 'IA' and Cash_Category_VC = 'IA_Int' and
 Period_TI = 9 and Year_SI = 2007 then Journal_T.Amount_NU else 0
end,
 case when Cash_Type_VC = 'IA' and Cash_Category_VC = 'IA_Int' and
 Period_TI = 10 and Year_SI = 2007 then Journal_T.Amount_NU else 0
end,
 case when Cash_Type_VC = 'IA' and Cash_Category_VC = 'IA_Int' and
 Period_TI = 11 and Year_SI = 2007 then Journal_T.Amount_NU else U
end,
 case when Cash_Type_VC = 'IA' and Cash_Category_VC = 'IA_Int' and
 Period_TI = 12 and Year_SI = 2007 then Journal_T.Amount_NU else 0
end,
 case when Cash_Type_VC = 'IA' and Cash_Category_VC = 'IA_Int' and
 Year_SI = 2007 then Journal_T.Amount_NU else 0 end
```

```
from Cash_T join Journal_T on
Cash_T.Doc_No_VC = Journal_T.Doc_No_VC
where  Cash_Type_VC = 'IA'  and  Cash_Category_VC = 'IA_Int'  and
Year_SI = 2007 and GL_ID = 2002

union all

select 'Net Cash Flow from Investing Activities',
 sum(case when Cash_Type_VC = 'IA' and Cash_Category_VC in
 ('IA_Pur','IA_Pro','IA_Int')and Period_TI = 1 and Year_SI = 2007
and
 GL_ID = 2002 then Journal_T.Amount_NU else 0 end),
 sum(case when Cash_Type_VC = 'IA' and Cash_Category_VC in
 ('IA_Pur','IA_Pro','IA_Int')and Period_TI = 2 and Year_SI = 2007
and
 GL_ID = 2002 then Journal_T.Amount_NU else 0 end),
 sum(case when Cash_Type_VC = 'IA' and Cash_Category_VC in
 ('IA_Pur','IA_Pro','IA_Int')and Period_TI = 3 and Year_SI = 2007
and
 GL_ID = 2002 then Journal_T.Amount_NU else 0 end),
 sum(case when Cash_Type_VC = 'IA' and Cash_Category_VC in
 ('IA_Pur','IA_Pro','IA_Int')and Period_TI = 4 and Year_SI = 2007
and
 GL_ID = 2002 then Journal_T.Amount_NU else 0 end),
 sum(case when Cash_Type_VC = 'IA' and Cash_Category_VC in
 ('IA_Pur','IA_Pro','IA_Int')and Period_TI = 5 and Year_SI = 2007
and
 GL_ID = 2002 then Journal_T.Amount_NU else 0 end),
 sum(case when Cash_Type_VC = 'IA' and Cash_Category_VC in
 ('IA_Pur','IA_Pro','IA_Int')and Period_TI = 6 and Year_SI = 2007
and
 GL_ID = 2002 then Journal_T.Amount_NU else 0 end),
 sum(case when Cash_Type_VC = 'IA' and Cash_Category_VC in
 ('IA_Pur','IA_Pro','IA_Int')and Period_TI = 7 and Year_SI = 2007
and
 GL_ID = 2002 then Journal_T.Amount_NU else 0 end),
 sum(case when Cash_Type_VC = 'IA' and Cash_Category_VC in
 ('IA_Pur','IA_Pro','IA_Int')and Period_TI = 8 and Year_SI = 2007
and
 GL_ID = 2002 then Journal_T.Amount_NU else 0 end),
 sum(case when Cash_Type_VC = 'IA' and Cash_Category_VC in
 ('IA_Pur','IA_Pro','IA_Int')and Period_TI = 9 and Year_SI = 2007
and
 GL_ID = 2002 then Journal_T.Amount_NU else 0 end),
 sum(case when Cash_Type_VC = 'IA' and Cash_Category_VC in
 ('IA_Pur','IA_Pro','IA_Int')and Period_TI = 10 and Year_SI = 2007
and
 GL_ID = 2002 then Journal_T.Amount_NU else 0 cnd),
 sum(case when Cash_Type_VC = 'IA' and Cash_Category_VC in
 ('IA_Pur','IA_Pro','IA_Int')and Period_TI = 11 and Year_SI = 2007
and
 GL_ID = 2002 then Journal_T.Amount_NU else 0 end),
```

```
 sum(case when Cash_Type_VC = 'IA' and Cash_Category_VC in
 ('IA_Pur','IA_Pro','IA_Int')and Period_TI = 12 and Year_SI = 2007
and
 GL_ID = 2002 then Journal_T.Amount_NU else 0 end),
 sum(case when Cash_Type_VC = 'IA' and Cash_Category_VC in
 ('IA_Pur','IA_Pro','IA_Int')and Year_SI = 2007 and GL_ID = 2002
 then Journal_T.Amount_NU else 0 end)

from Cash_T join Journal_T on
Cash_T.Doc_No_VC = Journal_T.Doc_No_VC

union all

select 'Cash from Financing Activities :' as [Cash Flow],
 sum(case when Cash_Type_VC = 'aaa' then
 Amount_NU else 0 end) as [Period 01],
 sum(case when Cash_Type_VC = 'aaa' then
 Amount_NU else 0 end) as [Period 02],
 sum(case when Cash_Type_VC = 'aaa' then
 Amount_NU else 0 end) as [Period 03],
 sum(case when Cash_Type_VC = 'aaa' then
 Amount_NU else 0 end) as [Period 04],
 sum(case when Cash_Type_VC = 'aaa' then
 Amount_NU else 0 end) as [Period 05],
 sum(case when Cash_Type_VC = 'aaa' then
 Amount_NU else 0 end) as [Period 06],
 sum(case when Cash_Type_VC = 'aaa' then
 Amount_NU else 0 end) as [Period 07],
 sum(case when Cash_Type_VC = 'aaa' then
 Amount_NU else 0 end) as [Period 08],
 sum(case when Cash_Type_VC = 'aaa' then
 Amount_NU else 0 end) as [Period 09],
 sum(case when Cash_Type_VC = 'aaa' then
 Amount_NU else 0 end) as [Period 10],
 sum(case when Cash_Type_VC = 'aaa' then
 Amount_NU else 0 end) as [Period 11],
 sum(case when Cash_Type_VC = 'aaa' then
 Amount_NU else 0 end) as [Period 12],
 sum(case when Cash_Type_VC = 'aaa' then
 Amount_NU else 0 end) as [YTD]

from Cash_T join Journal_T on
Cash_T.Doc_No_VC = Journal_T.Doc_No_VC

union all

select Descrip_VC,
 case when Cash_Type_VC = 'FA' and Cash_Category_VC = 'FA_Cap' and
 Period_TI = 1 and Year_SI = 2007 then Journal_T.Amount_NU else 0
end,
 case when Cash_Type_VC = 'FA' and Cash_Category_VC = 'FA_Cap' and
```

```sql
 Period_TI = 2 and Year_SI = 2007 then Journal_T.Amount_NU else 0
end,
 case when Cash_Type_VC = 'FA' and Cash_Category_VC = 'FA_Cap' and
 Period_TI = 3 and Year_SI = 2007 then Journal_T.Amount_NU else 0
end,
 case when Cash_Type_VC = 'FA' and Cash_Category_VC = 'FA_Cap' and
 Period_TI = 4 and Year_SI = 2007 then Journal_T.Amount_NU else 0
end,
 case when Cash_Type_VC = 'FA' and Cash_Category_VC = 'FA_Cap' and
 Period_TI = 5 and Year_SI = 2007 then Journal_T.Amount_NU else 0
end,
 case when Cash_Type_VC = 'FA' and Cash_Category_VC = 'FA_Cap' and
 Period_TI = 6 and Year_SI = 2007 then Journal_T.Amount_NU else 0
end,
 case when Cash_Type_VC = 'FA' and Cash_Category_VC = 'FA_Cap' and
 Period_TI = 7 and Year_SI = 2007 then Journal_T.Amount_NU else 0
end,
 case when Cash_Type_VC = 'FA' and Cash_Category_VC = 'FA_Cap' and
 Period_TI = 8 and Year_SI = 2007 then Journal_T.Amount_NU else 0
end,
 case when Cash_Type_VC = 'FA' and Cash_Category_VC = 'FA_Cap' and
 Period_TI = 9 and Year_SI = 2007 then Journal_T.Amount_NU else 0
end,
 case when Cash_Type_VC = 'FA' and Cash_Category_VC = 'FA_Cap' and
 Period_TI = 10 and Year_SI = 2007 then Journal_T.Amount_NU else 0
end,
 case when Cash_Type_VC = 'FA' and Cash_Category_VC = 'FA_Cap' and
 Period_TI = 11 and Year_SI = 2007 then Journal_T.Amount_NU else 0
end,

 case when Cash_Type_VC = 'FA' and Cash_Category_VC = 'FA_Cap' and
 Period_TI = 12 and Year_SI = 2007 then Journal_T.Amount_NU else 0
end,
 case when Cash_Type_VC = 'FA' and Cash_Category_VC = 'FA_Cap' and
 Year_SI = 2007 then Journal_T.Amount_NU else 0 end

from Cash_T join Journal_T on
Cash_T.Doc_No_VC = Journal_T.Doc_No_VC
where  Cash_Type_VC  =  'FA'  and  Cash_Category_VC  =  'FA_Cap'  and
Year_SI = 2007 and GL_ID = 2002

union all

select 'Net Cash Flow from Financing Activities',
 sum(case when Cash_Type_VC = 'FA' and Cash_Category_VC in
 ('FA_Cap')and Period_TI = 1 and Year_SI = 2007 and GL_ID = 2002
 then Journal_T.Amount_NU else 0 end),
 sum(case when Cash_Type_VC = 'FA' and Cash_Category_VC in
 ('FA_Cap')and Period_TI = 2 and Year_SI = 2007 and GL_ID = 2002
 then Journal_T.Amount_NU else 0 end),
 sum(case when Cash_Type_VC = 'FA' and Cash_Category_VC in
 ('FA_Cap')and Period_TI = 3 and Year_SI = 2007 and GL_ID = 2002
```

```
then Journal_T.Amount_NU else 0 end),
sum(case when Cash_Type_VC = 'FA' and Cash_Category_VC in
('FA_Cap')and Period_TI = 4 and Year_SI = 2007 and GL_ID = 2002
then Journal_T.Amount_NU else 0 end),
sum(case when Cash_Type_VC = 'FA' and Cash_Category_VC in
('FA_Cap')and Period_TI = 5 and Year_SI = 2007 and GL_ID = 2002
then Journal_T.Amount_NU else 0 end),
sum(case when Cash_Type_VC = 'FA' and Cash_Category_VC in
('FA_Cap')and Period_TI = 6 and Year_SI = 2007 and GL_ID = 2002
then Journal_T.Amount_NU else 0 end),
sum(case when Cash_Type_VC = 'FA' and Cash_Category_VC in
('FA_Cap')and Period_TI = 7 and Year_SI = 2007 and GL_ID = 2002
then Journal_T.Amount_NU else 0 end),
sum(case when Cash_Type_VC = 'FA' and Cash_Category_VC in
('FA_Cap')and Period_TI = 8 and Year_SI = 2007 and GL_ID = 2002
then Journal_T.Amount_NU else 0 end),
sum(case when Cash_Type_VC = 'FA' and Cash_Category_VC in
('FA_Cap')and Period_TI = 9 and Year_SI = 2007 and GL_ID = 2002
then Journal_T.Amount_NU else 0 end),
sum(case when Cash_Type_VC = 'FA' and Cash_Category_VC in
('FA_Cap')and Period_TI = 10 and Year_SI = 2007 and GL_ID = 2002
then Journal_T.Amount_NU else 0 end),
sum(case when Cash_Type_VC = 'FA' and Cash_Category_VC in
('FA_Cap')and Period_TI = 11 and Year_SI = 2007 and GL_ID = 2002
then Journal_T.Amount_NU else 0 end),
sum(case when Cash_Type_VC = 'FA' and Cash_Category_VC in
('FA_Cap')and Period_TI = 12 and Year_SI = 2007 and GL_ID = 2002
then Journal_T.Amount_NU else 0 end),
sum(case when Cash_Type_VC = 'FA' and Cash_Category_VC in
('FA_Cap')and Year_SI = 2007 and GL_ID = 2002
then Journal_T.Amount_NU else 0 end)

from Cash_T join Journal_T on
Cash_T.Doc_No_VC = Journal_T.Doc_No_VC


union all

select 'Net Increase/(Decrease) in Cash & Cash equivalent',
sum(case when Cash_Type_VC in ('OA','IA','FA') and Period_TI = 1
and
Year_SI = 2007 and GL_ID = 2002 then Journal_T.Amount_NU else 0
end),
sum(case when Cash_Type_VC in ('OA','IA','FA') and Period_TI = 2
and
Year_SI = 2007 and GL_ID = 2002 then Journal_T.Amount_NU else 0
end),
sum(case when Cash_Type_VC in ('OA','IA','FA') and Period_TI = 3
and
Year_SI = 2007 and GL_ID = 2002 then Journal_T.Amount_NU else 0
end),
```

```sql
sum(case when Cash_Type_VC in ('OA','IA','FA') and Period_TI = 4
and
 Year_SI = 2007 and GL_ID = 2002 then Journal_T.Amount_NU else 0
end),
 sum(case when Cash_Type_VC in ('OA','IA','FA') and Period_TI = 5
and
 Year_SI = 2007 and GL_ID = 2002 then Journal_T.Amount_NU else 0
end),
 sum(case when Cash_Type_VC in ('OA','IA','FA') and Period_TI = 6
and
 Year_SI = 2007 and GL_ID = 2002 then Journal_T.Amount_NU else 0
end),
 sum(case when Cash_Type_VC in ('OA','IA','FA') and Period_TI = 7
and
 Year_SI = 2007 and GL_ID = 2002 then Journal_T.Amount_NU else 0
end),
 sum(case when Cash_Type_VC in ('OA','IA','FA') and Period_TI = 8
and
 Year_SI = 2007 and GL_ID = 2002 then Journal_T.Amount_NU else 0
end),
 sum(case when Cash_Type_VC in ('OA','IA','FA') and Period_TI = 9
and
 Year_SI = 2007 and GL_ID = 2002 then Journal_T.Amount_NU else 0
end),
 sum(case when Cash_Type_VC in ('OA','IA','FA') and Period_TI = 10
and
 Year_SI = 2007 and GL_ID = 2002 then Journal_T.Amount_NU else 0
end),
 sum(case when Cash_Type_VC in ('OA','IA','FA') and Period_TI = 11
and
 Year_SI = 2007 and GL_ID = 2002 then Journal_T.Amount_NU else 0
end),
 sum(case when Cash_Type_VC in ('OA','IA','FA') and Period_TI = 12
and
 Year_SI = 2007 and GL_ID = 2002 then Journal_T.Amount_NU else 0
end),
 sum(case when Cash_Type_VC in ('OA','IA','FA')and Year_SI = 2007
and
 GL_ID = 2002 then Journal_T.Amount_NU else 0 end)

from Cash_T join Journal_T on
Cash_T.Doc_No_VC = Journal_T.Doc_No_VC
```

Now, test your query, by clicking on the parse query button to check for any syntax error, if your syntax is working, you would see the message "The command(s) completed successfully." Then, execute the query, by clicking on the execute query button, and you would see the following output appearing on your result pane.

Cash Flow	Period 06	Period 07	Period 08	Period 12	YTD
Cash from Operating Activities :	0	0	0	0	0
Receipt frm William	0	0	2000	0	2000
Receipt frm Randy	0	0	2000	0	2000
Cash generated from Operations	0	0	4000	0	4000
Payment of interest	0	0	0	-745	-745
Payment of taxes	0	-600	0	0	-600
Net Cash Flow from Operating Activities	0	-600	4000	-745	2655
Cash from Investing Activities :	0	0	0	0	0
Purchase FA	-1710	0	0	0	-1710
Interest from bank	0	250	0	0	250
Net Cash Flow from Investing Activities	-1710	250	0	0	-1460
Cash from Financing Activities :	0	0	0	0	0
Proceeds frm shares issue	0	0	2000	0	2000
Net Cash Flow from Financing Activities	0	0	2000	0	2000
Net Increase/(Decrease) in Cash & Cash equivalent	-1710	-350	6000	-745	3195

Now, we have a broader picture of MaxCorp's cash flow. The above result has been truncated to only show those columns that contain records. We can tell from the above result that, the receipt of $4000, is derived from William and Randy, collected in period 8. This is what Dave has requested initially, when we were designing and normalizing our Cash Table in Chapter 6.

How It Works – Select Query for Cash Flow Periodic Statement Report

Let us go through understanding the function of our first block of query. If you look closely to the code that we have just created, we are actually repeating the query when we first create our query for the Cash Flow Summary statement. We place the header name
'Cash from Operating Activities :' on our first column, then we place the figure 0, when the query failed to match the fictitious record that we specified as our filtering condition.
This applies across the rest of the column on the first row.

```
select 'Cash from Operating Activities :' as [Cash Flow],
 sum(case when Cash_Type_VC = 'aaa' then Journal_T.Amount_NU else
 0 end) as [Period 01],
 ;;;;;;;;;;;;;;;;;;;;;;;;;;;;;;;;;;;;;;;;;;;;;;;;;;;;;;;;;;;;;;;;;;
 ;;;;;;;;;;;;;;;;;;;;;;;;;;;;;;;;;;;;;;;;;;;;;;;;;;;;;;;;;;;;;;;;;;

 sum(case when Cash_Type_VC = 'aaa' then Journal_T.Amount_NU else
 0 end) as [Period 12],
 sum(case when Cash_Type_VC = 'aaa' then Journal_T.Amount_NU else
 0 end) as [YTD]

from Cash_T join Journal_T on
```

```
Cash_T.Doc_No_VC = Journal_T.Doc_No_VC
```

Next, we select receipt records from our Journal Table for the amount, from the Cash Table to filter only those with the cash type 'OA' and with category of 'OA_Deb'. We specify an additional filtering condition for the period. We then join the Cash Table and Journals Table together in our query.

```
union all

select Descrip_VC,
 case when Cash_Type_VC = 'OA' and Cash_Category_VC = 'OA_Deb' and
 Period_TI = 1 and Year_SI = 2007 then Journal_T.Amount_NU else 0
end,
;;;;;;;;;;;;;;;;;;;;;;;;;;;;;;;;;;;;;;;;;;;;;;;;;;;;;;;;;;;;;;;;
;;;;;;;;;;;;;;;;;;;;;;;;;;;;;;;;;;;;;;;;;;;;;;;;;;;;;;;;;;;;;;;;
;;;;;;
 case when Cash_Type_VC = 'OA' and Cash_Category_VC = 'OA_Deb' and
 Period_TI = 12 and Year_SI = 2007 then Journal_T.Amount_NU else 0
end,
 case when Cash_Type_VC = 'OA' and Cash_Category_VC = 'OA_Deb' and
 Year_SI = 2007 then Journal_T.Amount_NU else 0 end

from Cash_T join Journal_T on
Cash_T.Doc_No_VC = Journal_T.Doc_No_VC
where  Cash_Type_VC  =  'OA'  and  Cash_Category_VC  =  'OA_Deb'  and
Year_SI = 2007 and GL_ID = 2002
```

The remaining query, does the same function as explained earlier on our first block of query, we only specify the period required, as an additional filtering condition in the query.

4) Using SQL to produce Bank Reconciliation Statement

This statement would reconcile the balance between MaxCorp's bank account and its cash ledger. It basically add and minus some of the unmatchable records against its cash ledger balance, in arriving at its bank account balance. For this purpose, we would require MaxCorp's latest copy of its banker's statement. Let us create a table, and the necessary fields, before we begin inserting records into the table. We name this table, Bank_Statement.

Bank_Statement

	Column Name	Data Type	Length	Allow Nulls
	[Date]	smalldatetime	4	
	Chq_No	int	4	
	Detail	varchar	20	
	Amt	numeric	9	
	Period_TI	tinyint	1	
	Year_SI	smallint	2	

This is how; a normal bank statement would appear like, in reality.
Let us insert the following records into the Bank_Statement Table as follows ;

Bank_Statement

Date	Chq_No	Detail	Amt	Period_TI	Year_SI
2/2/2007	88258	Inward TT	-1400	2	2007
2/17/2007	740244	Chq clearance	1500	2	2007
8/26/2007	95454	Receipt frm William	-2000	8	2007
7/25/2007	44511	Interest from bank	-250	7	2007

Let us enter the following select query as follows

```
select convert(varchar,Date_DT,3) as [Date],Chq_No_VC,
 Descrip_VC as [Add Back Unpresented Cheques],
 case when Cash_T.Chq_No_VC Not in (Select Bank_Statement.Chq_No
 From Bank_Statement) and Journal_T.Amount_NU < 0 and GL_ID = 2002
 then Journal_T.Amount_NU*-1 else 0 end as [$]

from Cash_T join Journal_T on
Cash_T.Doc_No_VC = Journal_T.Doc_No_VC
where Cash_T.Chq_No_VC Not in (Select Bank_Statement.Chq_No From
Bank_Statement) and Journal_T.Amount_NU < 0 and GL_ID = 2002

select convert(varchar,Date_DT,3) as [Date],Chq_No_VC,
 Descrip_VC as [Less Amount not credited in Bank],
 case when Cash_T.Chq_No_VC Not in (Select Bank_Statement.Chq_No
 From Bank_Statement) and Journal_T.Amount_NU > 0 and GL_ID = 2002
 then Journal_T.Amount_NU*-1 else 0 end as [$]
from Cash_T join Journal_T on Cash_T.Doc_No_VC = Journal_T.Doc_No_VC
where Cash_T.Chq_No_VC Not in (Select Bank_Statement.Chq_No From
Bank_Statement) and Journal_T.Amount_NU > 0 and GL_ID = 2002

select convert(varchar,[Date],3) as [Date],Chq_No,
 Detail as [Add credited Amount not taken in GL],
 case when Bank_Statement.Chq_No Not in (Select Cash_T.Chq_No_VC
from    Cash_T    join    Journal_T    on    Cash_T.Doc_No_VC    =
Journal_T.Doc_No_VC) and Bank_Statement.Amt < 0
then Amt*-1 else 0 end as [$]
```

```
from Bank_Statement
where Bank_Statement.Chq_No Not in (Select Cash_T.Chq_No_VC from
Cash_T join Journal_T on Cash_T.Doc_No_VC = Journal_T.Doc_No_VC)
and Bank_Statement.Amt < 0

select convert(varchar,[Date],3) as [Date],Chq_No,
 Detail as [Less Amount debited not taken in GL],
 case when Bank_Statement.Chq_No Not in (Select Cash_T.Chq_No_VC
 From Cash_T join Journal_T on
 Cash_T.Doc_No_VC = Journal_T.Doc_No_VC) and Bank_Statement.Amt > 0
 then Amt*-1 else 0 end as [$]
from Bank_Statement
where Bank_Statement.Chq_No Not in (Select Cash_T.Chq_No_VC From
Cash_T join Journal_T on Cash_T.Doc_No_VC = Journal_T.Doc_No_VC)
and Bank_Statement.Amt > 0
```

Now, test your query, by clicking on the parse query button to check for any syntax error, if your syntax is working, you would see the message "The command(s) completed successfully." Then, execute the query, by clicking on the execute query button, and you would see the following output appearing on your result pane.

	Date	Chq_No_VC	Add Back Unpresented Cheques	$
1	26/12/07	745570	Payment of interest	745
2	25/07/07	745571	Payment of taxes	600
3	25/06/07	745571	Purchase FA	1710

	Date	Chq_No_VC	Less Amount not credited in Bank	$
1	25/08/07	8875	Proceeds frm shares issue	-2000
2	26/08/07	12454	Receipt frm Randy	-2000

	Date	Chq_No	Add credited Amount not taken in GL	$
1	02/02/07	88258	Inward TT	1400

	Date	Chq_No	Less Amount debited not taken in GL	$
1	17/02/07	740244	Chq clearance	-1500

We shall add and less all the amount as stated above on our result pane against the balance in our bank account code, 2002, and we would be able to reconcile the difference to MaxCorp's bank statement balance, as shown on the following working spreadsheet.

	A	B	C
1	Bank Reconciliation		
2			$
3	Bank Balance		3195
4			
5	Add Unpresented Cheques :		
6	26/12/2007	745570	745
7	25/07/2007	745571	600
8	25/06/2007	745571	1710
9			
10	Add Credited Amount not taken in GL		
11	02/02/2007	88258	1400
12			
13	Less Amount not credited in Bank		
14	25/08/2007	8875	-2000
15	26/08/2007	12454	-2000
16			
17			
18	Less Amount Debited not taken in GL		
19	17/02/2007	740244	-1500
20	Balance as per Bank Statement		2150

How It Works – Select Query for Bank Reconciliation Statement Report

Let us go through our first block of query. We change our date format to the one that we required, and place it on the first column; next, we place the cheque number on the second column, and the amount on the last column. We specify in our query, to filter out those payment records in the Cash Table, that are not in existence in the bank statement Table, by comparing the cheque number from both tables, and place them under the
header 'Add Back Unpresented Cheques'. We know, that, all the required fields, are located in Cash Table and Journal Table, thus, we join these table together.

```
select convert(varchar,Date_DT,3) as [Date],Chq_No_VC,
 Descrip_VC as [Add Back Unpresented Cheques],
 case when Cash_T.Chq_No_VC Not in (Select Bank_Statement.Chq_No
 From Bank_Statement) and Journal_T.Amount_NU < 0 and GL_ID = 2002
 then Journal_T.Amount_NU*-1 else 0 end as [$]

from Cash_T join Journal_T on
Cash_T.Doc_No_VC = Journal_T.Doc_No_VC
where  Cash_T.Chq_No_VC  Not  in  (Select  Bank_Statement.Chq_No  From
Bank_Statement) and Journal_T.Amount_NU < 0 and GL_ID = 2002
```

Next, in our second block of query, we call our query to filter out those collection records in the Cash Table, that are not in existence in the bank statement Table, by comparing the cheque number from both tables, and place them under the header 'Less Amount not credited in Bank'. We know, that, all the required fields, are located in Cash Table and Journal Table, thus, we join these table together.

```
select convert(varchar,Date_DT,3) as [Date],Chq_No_VC,
 Descrip_VC as [Less Amount not credited in Bank],
 case when Cash_T.Chq_No_VC Not in (Select Bank_Statement.Chq_No
 From Bank_Statement) and Journal_T.Amount_NU > 0 and GL_ID = 2002
 then Journal_T.Amount_NU*-1 else 0 end as [$]
from Cash_T join Journal_T on Cash_T.Doc_No_VC = Journal_T.Doc_No_VC
where Cash_T.Chq_No_VC Not in (Select Bank_Statement.Chq_No From
Bank_Statement) and Journal_T.Amount_NU > 0 and GL_ID = 2002
```

Then, in our third block of query, we call our query to filter out those cheque receipt records in the bank statement Table, that are not in existence in the Cash Table, by comparing the cheque number from both tables, and place them under the header 'Add credited Amount not taken in GL'. We know, that, all the required fields, are located in Cash Table and Journal Table, thus, we join these table together.

```
select convert(varchar,[Date],3) as [Date],Chq_No,
 Detail as [Add credited Amount not taken in GL],
 case when Bank_Statement.Chq_No Not in (Select Cash_T.Chq_No_VC
from     Cash_T     join     Journal_T     on     Cash_T.Doc_No_VC     =
Journal_T.Doc_No_VC) and Bank_Statement.Amt < 0
then Amt*-1 else 0 end as [$]

from Bank_Statement
where Bank_Statement.Chq_No Not in (Select Cash_T.Chq_No_VC from
Cash_T join Journal_T on Cash_T.Doc_No_VC = Journal_T.Doc_No_VC)
and Bank_Statement.Amt < 0
```

Finally, in our last block of query, we call our query to filter out those cheque payment records in the bank statement Table, that are not in existence in the Cash Table, by comparing the cheque number from both tables, and place them under the header 'Less Amount debited not taken in GL'. We know, that, all the required fields, are located in Cash Table and Journal Table, thus, we join these table together.

```
select convert(varchar,[Date],3) as [Date],Chq_No,
 Detail as [Less Amount debited not taken in GL],
 case when Bank_Statement.Chq_No Not in (Select Cash_T.Chq_No_VC
 From Cash_T join Journal_T on
 Cash_T.Doc_No_VC = Journal_T.Doc_No_VC) and Bank_Statement.Amt > 0
 then Amt*-1 else 0 end as [$] from Bank_Statement
where Bank_Statement.Chq_No Not in (Select Cash_T.Chq_No_VC From
Cash_T join Journal_T on Cash_T.Doc_No_VC = Journal_T.Doc_No_VC)
and Bank_Statement.Amt > 0
```

Summary

In Chapter 12, we have learned how to create reports from the Cash Table, applying the Transact-SQL to perform the select query to produce the necessary accounting reports required by MaxCorp.

To summarize, in this chapter, we have discussed:

- ➢ How to create select query to produce a Cash Flow Forecast

- ➢ How to create select query to produce a Cash Flow Summary Statement

- ➢ How to create select query to produce a Cash Flow Periodic Statement

- ➢ How to create select query to produce a Bank Reconciliation Statement

Chapter 13

Creating Reports from Asset Table

In this Chapter, we will be learning how, we can generate query to produce the following reports as requested by Dave in Chapter 7.

1) Asset Summary
2) Asset Movement Report

1) Using SQL to produce Asset Summary

This is a summary of asset movement, showing asset addition and disposal within a year, for each asset type, in terms of cost and accumulated depreciation. Let us enter the following records in the Fixed Asset Table as follows.

FixedAsset_T				
FA_ID_IN	FA_Type_VC	FA_Category_VC	FA_Descrip_VC	Doc_No_VC
100	CE	Deprn	Deprn	JV1012
100	CE	DispCost	DispCost	JV1011
100	CE	DispDeprn	DispDeprn	JV1011
101	OE	Cost	OfficeEquip	JV1010
101	OE	Deprn	Deprn	JV1012
101	OE	DispCost	DispCost	JV1011
101	OE	DispDeprn	DispDeprn	JV1011
102	FF	Cost	Furniture	JV1010
102	FF	Deprn	Deprn	JV1012
102	FF	DispCost	DispCost	JV1011
102	FF	DispDeprn	DispDeprn	JV1011
100	CE	Cost	CompEquip	JV1013
100	CE	Deprn	Deprn	JV1014
100	CE	DispCost	DispCost	JV1015
100	CE	DispDeprn	DispDeprn	JV1016
101	OE	Cost	OfficeEquip	JV1013
101	OE	Deprn	Deprn	JV1014
101	OE	DispCost	DispCost	JV1015
101	OE	DispDeprn	DispDeprn	JV1016
102	FF	Cost	Furniture	JV1013
102	FF	Deprn	Deprn	JV1014
102	FF	DispCost	DispCost	JV1015
102	FF	DispDeprn	DispDeprn	JV1016
100	CE	Cost	CompEquip	JV1010

Now, let us enter the following select query as follows

```
select 'Opening Balance' as [Cost],
 sum(case when FA_ID_IN = 100 and Descrip_VC in
 ('Purchase CompEquip','CE DispCost')
 and Year_SI < 2007 and GL_ID = 1000 and FA_Category_VC in
 ('Cost','DispCost')then Amount_NU else 0 end) as [CE],
 sum(case when FA_ID_IN = 101 and Descrip_VC in
 ('Purchase OfficeEquip','OE DispCost')
 and Year_SI < 2007 and GL_ID = 1000 and FA_Category_VC in
 ('Cost','DispCost')then Amount_NU else 0 end) as [OE],
 sum(case when FA_ID_IN = 102 and Descrip_VC in ('Purchase
 Furniture','FF DispCost')
 and Year_SI < 2007 and GL_ID = 1000 and FA_Category_VC in
 ('Cost','DispCost')then Amount_NU else 0 end) as [FF],

 sum(case when FA_ID_IN = 100 and Descrip_VC in
 ('Purchase CompEquip','CE DispCost')and Year_SI < 2007 and
 GL_ID = 1000 and FA_Category_VC in ('Cost','DispCost')
 then Amount_NU else 0 end) +
 sum(case when FA_ID_IN = 101 and Descrip_VC in
 ('Purchase OfficeEquip','OE DispCost')
 and Year_SI < 2007 and GL_ID = 1000 and FA_Category_VC in
 ('Cost','DispCost')then Amount_NU else 0 end) +
 sum(case when FA_ID_IN = 102 and Descrip_VC in

 ('Purchase Furniture','FF DispCost')
 and Year_SI < 2007 and GL_ID = 1000 and FA_Category_VC in
 ('Cost','DispCost')then Amount_NU else 0 end) as [Total]

from FixedAsset_T join Journal_T on
FixedAsset_T.Doc_No_VC = Journal_T.Doc_No_VC

union all

select 'Addition' as [Description],
 sum(case  when  FA_ID_IN  =  100  and  Descrip_VC  in  ('Purchase
CompEquip')
 and Year_SI = 2007 and GL_ID = 1000 and FA_Category_VC in ('Cost')
 then Amount_NU else 0 end) as [CE],
 sum(case when FA_ID_IN = 101 and Descrip_VC in
 ('Purchase OfficeEquip')and Year_SI = 2007 and GL_ID = 1000 and
 FA_Category_VC in ('Cost')then Amount_NU else 0 end) as [OE],
 sum(case  when  FA_ID_IN  =  102  and  Descrip_VC  in  ('Purchase
Furniture')
 and Year_SI = 2007 and GL_ID = 1000 and FA_Category_VC in ('Cost')
 then Amount_NU else 0 end) as [FF],
 sum(case  when  FA_ID_IN  =  100  and  Descrip_VC  in  ('Purchase
CompEquip')
 and Year_SI = 2007 and GL_ID = 1000 and FA_Category_VC in ('Cost')
 then Amount_NU else 0 end) +
```

```sql
sum(case when FA_ID_IN = 101 and Descrip_VC in
('Purchase OfficeEquip')and Year_SI = 2007 and GL_ID = 1000 and
FA_Category_VC in ('Cost') then Amount_NU else 0 end) +
sum(case when FA_ID_IN = 102 and Descrip_VC in ('Purchase
Furniture')
and Year_SI = 2007 and GL_ID = 1000 and FA_Category_VC in ('Cost')
then Amount_NU else 0 end)

from FixedAsset_T join Journal_T on
FixedAsset_T.Doc_No_VC = Journal_T.Doc_No_VC

union all

select 'Disposal' as [Description],
sum(case when FA_ID_IN = 100 and Descrip_VC in ('CE DispCost')
and Year_SI = 2007 and GL_ID = 1000 and FA_Category_VC in
('DispCost')
then Amount_NU else 0 end) as [CE],
sum(case when FA_ID_IN = 101 and Descrip_VC in ('OE DispCost')
and Year_SI = 2007 and GL_ID = 1000 and FA_Category_VC in
('DispCost')
then Amount_NU else 0 end) as [OE],
sum(case when FA_ID_IN = 102 and Descrip_VC in ('FF DispCost')
and Year_SI = 2007 and GL_ID = 1000 and FA_Category_VC in
('DispCost')
then Amount_NU else 0 end) as [FF],
sum(case when FA_ID_IN = 100 and Descrip_VC in ('CE DispCost')
and Year_SI = 2007 and GL_ID = 1000 and FA_Category_VC in
('DispCost')
then Amount_NU else 0 end) +
sum(case when FA_ID_IN = 101 and Descrip_VC in ('OE DispCost')
and Year_SI = 2007 and GL_ID = 1000 and FA_Category_VC in
('DispCost')
then Amount_NU else 0 end) +
sum(case when FA_ID_IN = 102 and Descrip_VC in ('FF DispCost')
and Year_SI = 2007 and GL_ID = 1000 and FA_Category_VC in
('DispCost')
then Amount_NU else 0 end)

from FixedAsset_T join Journal_T on
FixedAsset_T.Doc_No_VC = Journal_T.Doc_No_VC

union all

select 'Closing Balance',
sum(case when FA_ID_IN = 100 and Descrip_VC in
('Purchase CompEquip','CE DispCost')
and Year_SI < 2007 and GL_ID = 1000 and FA_Category_VC in
('Cost','DispCost')then Amount_NU else 0 end) +
sum(case when FA_ID_IN = 100 and Descrip_VC in
('Purchase CompEquip','CE DispCost')and Year_SI = 2007 and
GL_ID = 1000 and FA_Category_VC in ('Cost','DispCost')
```

```sql
then Amount_NU else 0 end) as [CE],
sum(case when FA_ID_IN = 101 and Descrip_VC in
('Purchase OfficeEquip','OE DispCost')
and Year_SI < 2007 and GL_ID = 1000 and FA_Category_VC in
('Cost','DispCost')then Amount_NU else 0 end) +
sum(case when FA_ID_IN = 101 and Descrip_VC in ('Purchase
OfficeEquip','OE DispCost')and Year_SI = 2007 and GL_ID = 1000 and
FA_Category_VC in ('Cost','DispCost')then
Amount_NU else 0 end) as [OE],
sum(case when FA_ID_IN = 102 and Descrip_VC in
('Purchase Furniture','FF DispCost')and Year_SI < 2007 and
GL_ID = 1000 and FA_Category_VC in ('Cost','DispCost')
then Amount_NU else 0 end) +
sum(case when FA_ID_IN = 102 and Descrip_VC in
('Purchase Furniture','FF DispCost')and Year_SI = 2007 and
GL_ID = 1000 and FA_Category_VC in ('Cost','DispCost')
then Amount_NU else 0 end) as [FF],
sum(case when FA_ID_IN = 100 and Descrip_VC in
('Purchase CompEquip','CE DispCost')and Year_SI < 2007 and
GL_ID = 1000 and FA_Category_VC in ('Cost','DispCost')
then Amount_NU else 0 end) +
sum(case when FA_ID_IN = 101 and Descrip_VC in
('Purchase OfficeEquip','OE DispCost')and Year_SI < 2007 and
GL_ID = 1000 and FA_Category_VC in ('Cost','DispCost')
then Amount_NU else 0 end) +
sum(case when FA_ID_IN = 102 and Descrip_VC in
('Purchase Furniture','FF DispCost')and Year_SI < 2007 and
GL_ID = 1000 and FA_Category_VC in ('Cost','DispCost')
then Amount_NU else 0 end) +
sum(case when FA_ID_IN = 100 and Descrip_VC in
('Purchase CompEquip','CE DispCost')and Year_SI = 2007 and
GL_ID = 1000 and FA_Category_VC in ('Cost','DispCost')
then Amount_NU else 0 end) +
sum(case when FA_ID_IN = 101 and Descrip_VC in
('Purchase OfficeEquip','OE DispCost')and Year_SI = 2007 and
GL_ID = 1000 and FA_Category_VC in ('Cost','DispCost')
then Amount_NU else 0 end) +
sum(case when FA_ID_IN = 102 and Descrip_VC in
('Purchase Furniture','FF DispCost')and Year_SI = 2007 and
GL_ID = 1000 and FA_Category_VC in ('Cost','DispCost')
then Amount_NU else 0 end) as [Total]

from FixedAsset_T join Journal_T on
FixedAsset_T.Doc_No_VC = Journal_T.Doc_No_VC

select 'Opening Balance' as [Acc Deprn],
 sum(case when FA_ID_IN = 100 and Descrip_VC in
 ('CE Deprn','CE DispDeprn')
 and Year_SI < 2007 and GL_ID = 1001 and FA_Category_VC in
 ('Deprn','DispDeprn')then Amount_NU else 0 end) as [CE],
 sum(case when FA_ID_IN = 101 and Descrip_VC in
 ('OE Deprn','OE DispDeprn')
```

```sql
and Year_SI < 2007 and GL_ID = 1001 and FA_Category_VC in
('Deprn','DispDeprn')then Amount_NU else 0 end) as [OE],
sum(case when FA_ID_IN = 102 and Descrip_VC in
('FF Deprn','FF DispDeprn')
and Year_SI < 2007 and GL_ID = 1001 and FA_Category_VC in
('Deprn','DispDeprn')then Amount_NU else 0 end) as [FF],
sum(case when FA_ID_IN = 100 and Descrip_VC in
('CE Deprn','CE DispDeprn')
and Year_SI < 2007 and GL_ID = 1001 and FA_Category_VC in
('Deprn','DispDeprn')then Amount_NU else 0 end) +
sum(case when FA_ID_IN = 101 and Descrip_VC in
('OE Deprn','OE DispDeprn')
and Year_SI < 2007 and GL_ID = 1001 and FA_Category_VC in
('Deprn','DispDeprn')then Amount_NU else 0 end) +
sum(case when FA_ID_IN = 102 and Descrip_VC in
('FF Deprn','FF DispDeprn')
and Year_SI < 2007 and GL_ID = 1001 and FA_Category_VC in
('Deprn','DispDeprn')then Amount_NU else 0 end) as [Total]

from FixedAsset_T join Journal_T on
FixedAsset_T.Doc_No_VC = Journal_T.Doc_No_VC

union all

select 'Addition' as [Description],
 sum(case when FA_ID_IN = 100 and Descrip_VC in ('CE Deprn')
 and Year_SI = 2007 and GL_ID = 1001 and FA_Category_VC in ('Deprn')
 then Amount_NU else 0 end) as [CE],
 sum(case when FA_ID_IN = 101 and Descrip_VC in ('OE Deprn')
 and Year_SI = 2007 and GL_ID = 1001 and FA_Category_VC in ('Deprn')
 then Amount_NU else 0 end) as [OE],
 sum(case when FA_ID_IN = 102 and Descrip_VC in ('FF Deprn')
 and Year_SI = 2007 and GL_ID = 1001 and FA_Category_VC in ('Deprn')
 then Amount_NU else 0 end) as [FF],
 sum(case when FA_ID_IN = 100 and Descrip_VC in ('CE Deprn')
 and Year_SI = 2007 and GL_ID = 1001 and FA_Category_VC in ('Deprn')
 then Amount_NU else 0 end) +
 sum(case when FA_ID_IN = 101 and Descrip_VC in ('OE Deprn')
 and Year_SI = 2007 and GL_ID = 1001 and FA_Category_VC in ('Deprn')
 then Amount_NU else 0 end) +
 sum(case when FA_ID_IN = 102 and Descrip_VC in ('FF Deprn')
 and Year_SI = 2007 and GL_ID = 1001 and FA_Category_VC in ('Deprn')
 then Amount_NU else 0 end)

from FixedAsset_T join Journal_T on
FixedAsset_T.Doc_No_VC = Journal_T.Doc_No_VC

union all

select 'Disposal' as [Description],
 sum(case when FA_ID_IN = 100 and Descrip_VC in ('CE DispDeprn')
 and Year_SI = 2007 and GL_ID = 1001 and FA_Category_VC in
```

```
    ('DispDeprn')then Amount_NU else 0 end) as [CE],
    sum(case when FA_ID_IN = 101 and Descrip_VC in ('OE DispDeprn')
    and Year_SI = 2007 and GL_ID = 1001 and FA_Category_VC in
    ('DispDeprn')then Amount_NU else 0 end) as [OE],
    sum(case when FA_ID_IN = 102 and Descrip_VC in ('FF DispDeprn')
    and Year_SI = 2007 and GL_ID = 1001 and FA_Category_VC in
    ('DispDeprn')then Amount_NU else 0 end) as [FF],
    sum(case when FA_ID_IN = 100 and Descrip_VC in ('CE DispDeprn')
    and Year_SI = 2007 and GL_ID = 1001 and FA_Category_VC in
    ('DispDeprn')then Amount_NU else 0 end) +
    sum(case when FA_ID_IN = 101 and Descrip_VC in ('OE DispDeprn')
    and Year_SI = 2007 and GL_ID = 1001 and FA_Category_VC in
    ('DispDeprn')then Amount_NU else 0 end) +
    sum(case when FA_ID_IN = 102 and Descrip_VC in ('FF DispDeprn')
    and Year_SI = 2007 and GL_ID = 1001 and FA_Category_VC in
    ('DispDeprn')then Amount_NU else 0 end)

from FixedAsset_T join Journal_T on
FixedAsset_T.Doc_No_VC = Journal_T.Doc_No_VC
union all

select 'Closing Balance',
 sum(case when FA_ID_IN = 100 and Descrip_VC in
 ('CE Deprn','CE DispDeprn')
 and Year_SI < 2007 and GL_ID = 1001 and FA_Category_VC in
 ('Deprn','DispDeprn')then Amount_NU else 0 end) +
 sum(case when FA_ID_IN = 100 and Descrip_VC in
 ('CE Deprn','CE DispDeprn')
 and Year_SI = 2007 and GL_ID = 1001 and FA_Category_VC in
 ('Deprn','DispDeprn')then Amount_NU else 0 end) as [CE],
 sum(case when FA_ID_IN = 101 and Descrip_VC in
 ('OE Deprn','OE DispDeprn')and Year_SI < 2007 and GL_ID = 1001 and
 FA_Category_VC in ('Deprn','DispDeprn')then Amount_NU else 0 end) +
 sum(case when FA_ID_IN = 101 and Descrip_VC in
 ('OE Deprn','OE DispDeprn')
 and Year_SI = 2007 and GL_ID = 1001 and FA_Category_VC in
 ('Deprn','DispDeprn')then Amount_NU else 0 end) as [OE],
 sum(case when FA_ID_IN = 102 and Descrip_VC in
 ('FF Deprn','FF DispDeprn')
 and Year_SI < 2007 and GL_ID = 1001 and FA_Category_VC in
 ('Deprn','DispDeprn')then Amount_NU else 0 end) +
 sum(case when FA_ID_IN = 102 and Descrip_VC in
 ('FF Deprn','FF DispDeprn')
 and Year_SI = 2007 and GL_ID = 1001 and FA_Category_VC in
 ('Deprn','DispDeprn')then Amount_NU else 0 end) as [FF],
 sum(case when FA_ID_IN = 100 and Descrip_VC in
 ('CE Deprn','CE DispDeprn')
 and Year_SI < 2007 and GL_ID = 1001 and FA_Category_VC in
 ('Deprn','DispDeprn')then Amount_NU else 0 end) +
 sum(case when FA_ID_IN = 101 and Descrip_VC in
 ('OE Deprn','OE DispDeprn')
```

```
and Year_SI < 2007 and GL_ID = 1001 and FA_Category_VC in
('Deprn','DispDeprn')then Amount_NU else 0 end) +
sum(case when FA_ID_IN = 102 and Descrip_VC in
('FF Deprn','FF DispDeprn')
and Year_SI < 2007 and GL_ID = 1001 and FA_Category_VC in
('Deprn','DispDeprn')then Amount_NU else 0 end) +
sum(case when FA_ID_IN = 100 and Descrip_VC in
('CE Deprn','CE DispDeprn')
and Year_SI = 2007 and GL_ID = 1001 and FA_Category_VC in
('Deprn','DispDeprn')then Amount_NU else 0 end) +
sum(case when FA_ID_IN = 101 and Descrip_VC in
('OE Deprn','OE DispDeprn')
and Year_SI = 2007 and GL_ID = 1001 and FA_Category_VC in
('Deprn','DispDeprn')then Amount_NU else 0 end) +
sum(case when FA_ID_IN = 102 and Descrip_VC in
('FF Deprn','FF DispDeprn')
and Year_SI = 2007 and GL_ID = 1001 and FA_Category_VC in
('Deprn','DispDeprn')then Amount_NU else 0 end) as [Total]

from FixedAsset_T join Journal_T on
FixedAsset_T.Doc_No_VC = Journal_T.Doc_No_VC
```

Now, test your query, by clicking on the parse query button to check for any syntax error, if your syntax is working, you would see the message "The command(s) completed successfully." Then, execute the query, by clicking on the execute query button, and you would see the following output appearing on your result pane.

	Cost	CE	OE	OE	Total
1	Opening Balance	400	500	550	1450
2	Addition	800	450	360	1610
3	Disposal	-50	-100	-10	-160
4	Closing Balance	1150	850	900	2900

	Acc Deprn	CE	OE	OE	Total
1	Opening Balance	-250	-300	-155	-705
2	Addition	-200	-120	-55	-375
3	Disposal	20	55	5	80
4	Closing Balance	-430	-365	-205	-1000

The total closing balance for cost and accumulated depreciation should tie to the asset element, contained in our balance sheet.

In our select query, we have broken down into two sections, the first section that will query for the cost element, second, and the depreciation element. Both queries perform the same function, so, we only need to analyze our first section, the cost element portion.

How It Works – Select Query for Asset Summary Report

Let us go through analyzing our first block of code. Our first block of query, will create a row for the opening balance. This row would contain all records captured in the Journals Table, before year 2007. We specify its asset category, asset id and its description for each of the asset category in our select query. Next, we create a calculated field to sum up the value across all three asset category, and place each amount on the Total column. We know, that, the fields we specified, is created from Journals Table and Fixed Asset Table, so, we join these two tables together.

```
select 'Opening Balance' as [Cost],
 sum(case when FA_ID_IN = 100 and Descrip_VC in
 ('Purchase CompEquip','CE DispCost')
 and Year_SI < 2007 and GL_ID = 1000 and FA_Category_VC in
 ('Cost','DispCost')then Amount_NU else 0 end) as [CE],
 sum(case when FA_ID_IN = 101 and Descrip_VC in
 ('Purchase OfficeEquip','OE DispCost')
 and Year_SI < 2007 and GL_ID = 1000 and FA_Category_VC in
 ('Cost','DispCost')then Amount_NU else 0 end) as [OE],
 sum(case when FA_ID_IN = 102 and Descrip_VC in
 ('Purchase Furniture','FF DispCost')
 and Year_SI < 2007 and GL_ID = 1000 and FA_Category_VC in
 ('Cost','DispCost')then Amount_NU else 0 end) as [FF],

 sum(case when FA_ID_IN = 100 and Descrip_VC in
 ('Purchase CompEquip','CE DispCost')and Year_SI < 2007 and
 GL_ID = 1000 and FA_Category_VC in ('Cost','DispCost')
 then Amount_NU else 0 end) +
 sum(case when FA_ID_IN = 101 and Descrip_VC in
 ('Purchase OfficeEquip','OE DispCost')
 and Year_SI < 2007 and GL_ID = 1000 and FA_Category_VC in
 ('Cost','DispCost')then Amount_NU else 0 end) +
 sum(case when FA_ID_IN = 102 and Descrip_VC in
 ('Purchase Furniture','FF DispCost')
 and Year_SI < 2007 and GL_ID = 1000 and FA_Category_VC in
 ('Cost','DispCost')then Amount_NU else 0 end) as [Total]

from FixedAsset_T join Journal_T on
FixedAsset_T.Doc_No_VC = Journal_T.Doc_No_VC
```

Next, we call our query to select records of asset purchased in year 2007, matching its description, its asset id and its asset category. We then, place the amount on their respective asset type column, under the Addition row. Again, we join the FixedAsset Table with the Journal Table.

```
union all

select 'Addition' as [Description],
 sum(case  when  FA_ID_IN  =  100  and  Descrip_VC  in  ('Purchase
CompEquip')
 and Year_SI = 2007 and GL_ID = 1000 and FA_Category_VC in ('Cost')
 then Amount_NU else 0 end) as [CE],
 sum(case when FA_ID_IN = 101 and Descrip_VC in

 ('Purchase OfficeEquip')and Year_SI = 2007 and GL_ID = 1000 and
 FA_Category_VC in ('Cost')then Amount_NU else 0 end) as [OE],
 sum(case when FA_ID_IN = 102 and Descrip_VC in
 ('Purchase Furniture')
 and Year_SI = 2007 and GL_ID = 1000 and FA_Category_VC in
 ('Cost')
 then Amount_NU else 0 end) as [FF],
 sum(case when FA_ID_IN = 100 and Descrip_VC in
 ('Purchase CompEquip')
 and Year_SI = 2007 and GL_ID = 1000 and FA_Category_VC in ('Cost')
 then Amount_NU else 0 end) +
 sum(case when FA_ID_IN = 101 and Descrip_VC in
 ('Purchase OfficeEquip')and Year_SI = 2007 and GL_ID = 1000 and
 FA_Category_VC in ('Cost') then Amount_NU else 0 end) +
 sum(case when FA_ID_IN = 102 and Descrip_VC in
 ('Purchase Furniture')
 and Year_SI = 2007 and GL_ID = 1000 and FA_Category_VC in ('Cost')
 then Amount_NU else 0 end)

from FixedAsset_T join Journal_T on
FixedAsset_T.Doc_No_VC = Journal_T.Doc_No_VC
```

Then, we create our next query, to select records of asset disposed in year 2007, matching its description, its asset id and its asset category. We then, place the amount on their respective asset type column, under the Disposal row. Then, we join the FixedAsset Table with the Journal Table.

```
union all

select 'Disposal' as [Description],
 sum(case when FA_ID_IN = 100 and Descrip_VC in ('CE DispDeprn')
 and Year_SI = 2007 and GL_ID = 1001 and FA_Category_VC in
 ('DispDeprn')then Amount_NU else 0 end) as [CE],
 sum(case when FA_ID_IN = 101 and Descrip_VC in ('OE DispDeprn')
 and Year_SI = 2007 and GL_ID = 1001 and FA_Category_VC in
 ('DispDeprn')then Amount_NU else 0 end) as [OE],
 sum(case when FA_ID_IN = 102 and Descrip_VC in ('FF DispDeprn')
 and Year_SI = 2007 and GL_ID = 1001 and FA_Category_VC in
 ('DispDeprn')then Amount_NU else 0 end) as [FF],
 sum(case when FA_ID_IN = 100 and Descrip_VC in ('CE DispDeprn')
 and Year_SI = 2007 and GL_ID = 1001 and FA_Category_VC in
 ('DispDeprn')then Amount_NU else 0 end) +
```

```
sum(case when FA_ID_IN = 101 and Descrip_VC in ('OE DispDeprn')
and Year_SI = 2007 and GL_ID = 1001 and FA_Category_VC in
('DispDeprn')then Amount_NU else 0 end) +
sum(case when FA_ID_IN = 102 and Descrip_VC in ('FF DispDeprn')
and Year_SI = 2007 and GL_ID = 1001 and FA_Category_VC in
('DispDeprn')then Amount_NU else 0 end)

from FixedAsset_T join Journal_T on
FixedAsset_T.Doc_No_VC = Journal_T.Doc_No_VC
union all
```

On the following query, we sum up all the records for purchase and disposal before and in year 2007, and place them under the closing balance row, for each asset type.

```
union all

select 'Closing Balance',
 sum(case when FA_ID_IN = 100 and Descrip_VC in
 ('Purchase CompEquip','CE DispCost')
 and Year_SI < 2007 and GL_ID = 1000 and FA_Category_VC in
 ('Cost','DispCost')then Amount_NU else 0 end) +
 sum(case when FA_ID_IN = 100 and Descrip_VC in
 ('Purchase CompEquip','CE DispCost')and Year_SI = 2007 and
 GL_ID = 1000 and FA_Category_VC in ('Cost','DispCost')
 then Amount_NU else 0 end) as [CE],
;;;;;;;;;;;;;;;;;;;;;;;;;;;;;;;;;;;;;;;;;;;;;;;;;;;;;;;;;;;;;;;;;;;;;;
;;;;;;;;;;;;;;;;;;;;;;;;;;;;;;;;;;;;;;;;;;;;;;;;;;;;;;;;;;;;;;;;;;;;;;
```

In our last block of query, we are summing up all the purchase and disposal records with the year before or equals to 2007, and place them on the Total column, under the closing balance row.

```
sum(case when FA_ID_IN = 100 and Descrip_VC in
('Purchase CompEquip','CE DispCost')and Year_SI < 2007 and
GL_ID = 1000 and FA_Category_VC in ('Cost','DispCost')
then Amount_NU else 0 end) +
sum(case when FA_ID_IN = 101 and Descrip_VC in
('Purchase OfficeEquip','OE DispCost')and Year_SI < 2007 and
GL_ID = 1000 and FA_Category_VC in ('Cost','DispCost')
then Amount_NU else 0 end) +
sum(case when FA_ID_IN = 102 and Descrip_VC in
('Purchase Furniture','FF DispCost')and Year_SI < 2007 and
GL_ID = 1000 and FA_Category_VC in ('Cost','DispCost')
then Amount_NU else 0 end) +
sum(case when FA_ID_IN = 100 and Descrip_VC in
('Purchase CompEquip','CE DispCost')and Year_SI = 2007 and
GL_ID = 1000 and FA_Category_VC in ('Cost','DispCost')
then Amount_NU else 0 end) +
sum(case when FA_ID_IN = 101 and Descrip_VC in
```

```
('Purchase OfficeEquip','OE DispCost')and Year_SI = 2007 and
GL_ID = 1000 and FA_Category_VC in ('Cost','DispCost')
then Amount_NU else 0 end) +
sum(case when FA_ID_IN = 102 and Descrip_VC in
('Purchase Furniture','FF DispCost')and Year_SI = 2007 and
GL_ID = 1000 and FA_Category_VC in ('Cost','DispCost')
then Amount_NU else 0 end) as [Total]

from FixedAsset_T join Journal_T on
FixedAsset_T.Doc_No_VC = Journal_T.Doc_No_VC
```

2) Using SQL to produce Asset Movement Report

This report is actually, an extension of the asset summary, breaking down the asset movement in periods, having the same layout format as the asset summary. We will create a select query for the asset type, computer equipment, specifically for this report.

Let us enter the following select query as follows

```
select FA_Type_VC + ' Addition' as [Cost Description],
 FA_ID_IN as [FA Code],
 sum(case when FA_Category_VC = 'Cost' and Period_TI = '1' and
 Year_SI = 2007 then Amount_NU else 0 end) as [Period 01],
 sum(case when FA_Category_VC = 'Cost' and Period_TI = '2' and
 Year_SI = 2007 then Amount_NU else 0 end) as [Period 02],
 sum(case when FA_Category_VC = 'Cost' and Period_TI = '3' and
 Year_SI = 2007 then Amount_NU else 0 end) as [Period 03],
 sum(case when FA_Category_VC = 'Cost' and Period_TI = '4' and
 Year_SI = 2007 then Amount_NU else 0 end) as [Period 04],
 sum(case when FA_Category_VC = 'Cost' and Period_TI = '5' and
 Year_SI = 2007 then Amount_NU else 0 end) as [Period 05],
 sum(case when FA_Category_VC = 'Cost' and Period_TI = '6' and
 Year_SI = 2007 then Amount_NU else 0 end) as [Period 06],
 sum(case when FA_Category_VC = 'Cost' and Period_TI = '7' and
 Year_SI = 2007 then Amount_NU else 0 end) as [Period 07],
 sum(case when FA_Category_VC = 'Cost' and Period_TI = '8' and
 Year_SI = 2007 then Amount_NU else 0 end) as [Period 08],
 sum(case when FA_Category_VC = 'Cost' and Period_TI = '9' and
 Year_SI = 2007 then Amount_NU else 0 end) as [Period 09],
 sum(case when FA_Category_VC = 'Cost' and Period_TI = '10' and
 Year_SI = 2007 then Amount_NU else 0 end) as [Period 10],
 sum(case when FA_Category_VC = 'Cost' and Period_TI = '11' and
 Year_SI = 2007 then Amount_NU else 0 end) as [Period 11],
 sum(case when FA_Category_VC = 'Cost' and Period_TI = '12' and
 Year_SI = 2007 then Amount_NU else 0 end) as [Period 12],
 sum(case when FA_Category_VC = 'Cost' and Year_ST = 2007
 then Amount_NU else 0 end) as [YTD]

from FixedAsset_T join Journal_T on
```

```
FixedAsset_T.Doc_No_VC = Journal_T.Doc_No_VC
where FA_Type_VC ='CE'
and Descrip_VC = 'Purchase CompEquip'
group by FA_Type_VC,FA_ID_IN

union all

select FA_Type_VC + ' Disposal' as [Description],FA_ID_IN,
 sum(case when FA_Category_VC = 'DispCost' and Period_TI = '1' and
 Year_SI = 2007 then Amount_NU else 0 end) as [Period 01],
 sum(case when FA_Category_VC = 'DispCost' and Period_TI = '2' and
 Year_SI = 2007 then Amount_NU else 0 end) as [Period 02],
 sum(case when FA_Category_VC = 'DispCost' and Period_TI = '3' and
 Year_SI = 2007 then Amount_NU else 0 end) as [Period 03],

 sum(case when FA_Category_VC = 'DispCost' and Period_TI = '4' and
 Year_SI = 2007 then Amount_NU else 0 end) as [Period 04],
 sum(case when FA_Category_VC = 'DispCost' and Period_TI = '5' and
 Year_SI = 2007 then Amount_NU else 0 end) as [Period 05],
 sum(case when FA_Category_VC = 'DispCost' and Period_TI = '6' and
 Year_SI = 2007 then Amount_NU else 0 end) as [Period 06],
 sum(case when FA_Category_VC = 'DispCost' and Period_TI = '7' and
 Year_SI = 2007 then Amount_NU else 0 end) as [Period 07],
 sum(case when FA_Category_VC = 'DispCost' and Period_TI = '8' and
 Year_SI = 2007 then Amount_NU else 0 end) as [Period 08],
 sum(case when FA_Category_VC = 'DispCost' and Period_TI = '9' and
 Year_SI = 2007 then Amount_NU else 0 end) as [Period 09],
 sum(case when FA_Category_VC = 'DispCost' and Period_TI = '10' and
 Year_SI = 2007 then Amount_NU else 0 end) as [Period 10],
 sum(case when FA_Category_VC = 'DispCost' and Period_TI = '11' and
 Year_SI = 2007 then Amount_NU else 0 end) as [Period 11],
 sum(case when FA_Category_VC = 'DispCost' and Period_TI = '12' and
 Year_SI = 2007 then Amount_NU else 0 end) as [Period 12],
 sum(case when FA_Category_VC = 'DispCost' and Year_SI = 2007
 then Amount_NU else 0 end) as [YTD]

 from FixedAsset_T join Journal_T on
 FixedAsset_T.Doc_No_VC = Journal_T.Doc_No_VC
 where FA_Type_VC ='CE'
 and Descrip_VC = 'CE DispCost'
 group by FA_Type_VC,FA_ID_IN

 union all

select FA_Type_VC + ' Net Cost' as [Description],FA_ID_IN,
 sum(case when FA_Category_VC in ('Cost','DispCost') and
 Period_TI = '1' and Year_SI = 2007
 then Amount_NU else 0 end) as [Period 01],
 sum(case when FA_Category_VC in ('Cost','DispCost') and
 Period_TI = '2' and Year_SI = 2007
 then Amount_NU else 0 end) as [Period 02],
 sum(case when FA_Category_VC in ('Cost','DispCost') and
```

```
          Period_TI = '3' and Year_SI = 2007
          then Amount_NU else 0 end) as [Period 03],
          sum(case when FA_Category_VC in ('Cost','DispCost') and
          Period_TI = '4' and Year_SI = 2007
          then Amount_NU else 0 end) as [Period 04],
          sum(case when FA_Category_VC in ('Cost','DispCost') and
          Period_TI = '5' and Year_SI = 2007
          then Amount_NU else 0 end) as [Period 05],
          sum(case when FA_Category_VC in ('Cost','DispCost') and
          Period_TI = '6' and Year_SI = 2007
          then Amount_NU else 0 end) as [Period 06],
          sum(case when FA_Category_VC in ('Cost','DispCost') and
          Period_TI = '7' and Year_SI = 2007
          then Amount_NU else 0 end) as [Period 07],
          sum(case when FA_Category_VC in ('Cost','DispCost') and
          Period_TI = '8' and Year_SI = 2007
          then Amount_NU else 0 end) as [Period 08],

          sum(case when FA_Category_VC in ('Cost','DispCost') and
          Period_TI = '9' and Year_SI = 2007
          then Amount_NU else 0 end) as [Period 09],
          sum(case when FA_Category_VC in ('Cost','DispCost') and
          Period_TI = '10' and Year_SI = 2007
          then Amount_NU else 0 end) as [Period 10],
          sum(case when FA_Category_VC in ('Cost','DispCost') and
          Period_TI = '11' and Year_SI = 2007
          then Amount_NU else 0 end) as [Period 11],
          sum(case when FA_Category_VC in ('Cost','DispCost') and
          Period_TI = '12' and Year_SI = 2007
          then Amount_NU else 0 end) as [Period 12],
          sum(case when FA_Category_VC in ('Cost','DispCost') and
          Year_SI = 2007 then Amount_NU else 0 end) as [YTD]

     from FixedAsset_T join Journal_T on
     FixedAsset_T.Doc_No_VC = Journal_T.Doc_No_VC
     where FA_Type_VC ='CE'
     and Descrip_VC in ('Purchase CompEquip','CE DispCost')
     group by FA_Type_VC,FA_ID_IN

     select FA_Type_VC + ' Addition' as [Deprn Description],
      FA_ID_IN as [FA Code],
      sum(case when FA_Category_VC = 'Deprn' and
      Period_TI = '1' and Year_SI = 2007
      then Amount_NU else 0 end) as [Period 01],
      sum(case when FA_Category_VC = 'Deprn' and
      Period_TI = '2' and Year_SI = 2007
      then Amount_NU else 0 end) as [Period 02],
      sum(case when FA_Category_VC = 'Deprn' and
      Period_TI = '3' and Year_SI = 2007
      then Amount_NU else 0 end) as [Period 03],
      sum(case when FA_Category_VC = 'Deprn' and
      Period_TI = '4' and Year_SI = 2007
```

```sql
then Amount_NU else 0 end) as [Period 04],
sum(case when FA_Category_VC = 'Deprn' and
Period_TI = '5' and Year_SI = 2007
then Amount_NU else 0 end) as [Period 05],
sum(case when FA_Category_VC = 'Deprn' and
Period_TI = '6' and Year_SI = 2007
then Amount_NU else 0 end) as [Period 06],
sum(case when FA_Category_VC = 'Deprn' and
Period_TI = '7' and Year_SI = 2007
then Amount_NU else 0 end) as [Period 07],
sum(case when FA_Category_VC = 'Deprn' and
Period_TI = '8' and Year_SI = 2007
then Amount_NU else 0 end) as [Period 08],
sum(case when FA_Category_VC = 'Deprn' and
Period_TI = '9' and Year_SI = 2007
then Amount_NU else 0 end) as [Period 09],
sum(case when FA_Category_VC = 'Deprn' and
Period_TI = '10' and Year_SI = 2007
then Amount_NU else 0 end) as [Period 10],

sum(case when FA_Category_VC = 'Deprn' and
Period_TI = '11' and Year_SI = 2007
then Amount_NU else 0 end) as [Period 11],
sum(case when FA_Category_VC = 'Deprn' and
Period_TI = '12' and Year_SI = 2007
then Amount_NU else 0 end) as [Period 12],
sum(case when FA_Category_VC = 'Deprn' and Year_SI = 2007
then Amount_NU else 0 end) as [YTD]

from FixedAsset_T join Journal_T on
FixedAsset_T.Doc_No_VC = Journal_T.Doc_No_VC
where FA_Type_VC ='CE'
and Descrip_VC in ('CE Deprn')
group by FA_Type_VC,FA_ID_IN

union all

select FA_Type_VC + ' Disposal' as [Description],FA_ID_IN,
sum(case when FA_Category_VC = 'DispDeprn' and
Period_TI = '1' and Year_SI = 2007
then Amount_NU else 0 end) as [Period 01],
sum(case when FA_Category_VC = 'DispDeprn' and
Period_TI = '2' and Year_SI = 2007
then Amount_NU else 0 end) as [Period 02],
sum(case when FA_Category_VC = 'DispDeprn' and
Period_TI = '3' and Year_SI = 2007
then Amount_NU else 0 end) as [Period 03],
sum(case when FA_Category_VC = 'DispDeprn' and
Period_TI = '4' and Year_SI = 2007
then Amount_NU else 0 end) as [Period 04],
sum(case when FA_Category_VC = 'DispDeprn' and
Period_TI = '5' and Year_SI = 2007
```

```
        then Amount_NU else 0 end) as [Period 05],
        sum(case when FA_Category_VC = 'DispDeprn' and
        Period_TI = '6' and Year_SI = 2007
        then Amount_NU else 0 end) as [Period 06],
        sum(case when FA_Category_VC = 'DispDeprn' and
        Period_TI = '7' and Year_SI = 2007
        then Amount_NU else 0 end) as [Period 07],
        sum(case when FA_Category_VC = 'DispDeprn' and
        Period_TI = '8' and Year_SI = 2007
        then Amount_NU else 0 end) as [Period 08],
        sum(case when FA_Category_VC = 'DispDeprn' and
        Period_TI = '9' and Year_SI = 2007
        then Amount_NU else 0 end) as [Period 09],
        sum(case when FA_Category_VC = 'DispDeprn' and
        Period_TI = '10' and Year_SI = 2007
        then Amount_NU else 0 end) as [Period 10],
        sum(case when FA_Category_VC = 'DispDeprn' and
        Period_TI = '11' and  Year_SI = 2007
        then Amount_NU else 0 end) as [Period 11],
        sum(case when FA_Category_VC = 'DispDeprn' and
        Period_TI = '12' and Year_SI = 2007
        then Amount_NU else 0 end) as [Period 12],
        sum(case when FA_Category_VC = 'DispDeprn' and Year_SI = 2007

        then Amount_NU else 0 end) as [YTD]

    from FixedAsset_T join Journal_T on
    FixedAsset_T.Doc_No_VC = Journal_T.Doc_No_VC
    where FA_Type_VC ='CE'
    and Descrip_VC in ('CE DispDeprn')
    group by FA_Type_VC,FA_ID_IN
    union all

    select FA_Type_VC + ' Net Deprn' as [Description],FA_ID_IN,
     sum(case when FA_Category_VC in ('Deprn','DispDeprn') and
     Period_TI = '1' and Year_SI = 2007
     then Amount_NU else 0 end) as [Period 01],
     sum(case when FA_Category_VC in ('Deprn','DispDeprn') and
     Period_TI = '2' and Year_SI = 2007
     then Amount_NU else 0 end) as [Period 02],
     sum(case when FA_Category_VC in ('Deprn','DispDeprn') and
     Period_TI = '3' and Year_SI = 2007
     then Amount_NU else 0 end) as [Period 03],
     sum(case when FA_Category_VC in ('Deprn','DispDeprn') and
     Period_TI = '4' and Year_SI = 2007
     then Amount_NU else 0 end) as [Period 04],
     sum(case when FA_Category_VC in ('Deprn','DispDeprn') and
     Period_TI = '5' and Year_SI = 2007
     then Amount_NU else 0 end) as [Period 05],
     sum(case when FA_Category_VC in ('Deprn','DispDeprn') and
     Period_TI = '6' and Year_SI = 2007
     then Amount_NU else 0 end) as [Period 06],
```

```
sum(case when FA_Category_VC in ('Deprn','DispDeprn') and
Period_TI = '7' and Year_SI = 2007
then Amount_NU else 0 end) as [Period 07],
sum(case when FA_Category_VC in ('Deprn','DispDeprn') and
Period_TI = '8' and Year_SI = 2007
then Amount_NU else 0 end) as [Period 08],
sum(case when FA_Category_VC in ('Deprn','DispDeprn') and
Period_TI = '9' and Year_SI = 2007
then Amount_NU else 0 end) as [Period 09],
sum(case when FA_Category_VC in ('Deprn','DispDeprn') and
Period_TI = '10' and Year_SI = 2007
then Amount_NU else 0 end) as [Period 10],
sum(case when FA_Category_VC in ('Deprn','DispDeprn') and
Period_TI = '11' and Year_SI = 2007
then Amount_NU else 0 end) as [Period 11],
sum(case when FA_Category_VC in ('Deprn','DispDeprn') and
Period_TI = '12' and Year_SI = 2007
then Amount_NU else 0 end) as [Period 12],
sum(case when FA_Category_VC in ('Deprn','DispDeprn') and
Year_SI = 2007
then Amount_NU else 0 end) as [YTD]

from FixedAsset_T join Journal_T on
FixedAsset_T.Doc_No_VC = Journal_T.Doc_No_VC
where FA_Type_VC ='CE'
and Descrip_VC in ('CE Deprn','CE DispDeprn')
group by FA_Type_VC,FA_ID_IN
```

Now, test your query, by clicking on the parse query button to check for any syntax error, if your syntax is working, you would see the message "The command(s) completed successfully." Then, execute the query, by clicking on the execute query button, and you would see the following output appearing on your result pane.

	Cost Description	FA Code	P.	Period 02	Period 06	Period 12	YTD
1	CE Addition	100	0	800	0	0	800
2	CE Disposal	100	0	0	−50	0	−50
3	CE Net Cost	100	0	800	−50	0	750

	Deprn Descrip...	FA Code	P.	Period 02	Period 06	Period 12	YTD
1	CE Addition	100	0	0	0	−200	−200
2	CE Disposal	100	0	0	20	0	20
3	CE Net Deprn	100	0	0	20	−200	−180

The above result has been customized to fit into our page width, for better view. We can analyze MaxCorp's asset movement more accurately now, if the addition and disposal category is broken down in periods.

How It Works – Select Query for Asset Movement Report

Let us look and analyze the function of our select query we have just created for the asset movement.

In our first block of query, we place the static text 'Addition' on the first column; next we place the asset id on the second column. We then pull and sum up the purchase records from the Journal Table, specifying the category name as 'Cost', and period as '1' in the year equals to 2007, and place it on the appropriate columns. We also need to specify the asset type and description, after joining the FixedAsset Table with the Journals Table, as we only want to extract the records that are related to computer equipment.

```
select FA_Type_VC + ' Addition' as [Cost Description],
 FA_ID_IN as [FA Code],
  sum(case when FA_Category_VC = 'Cost' and Period_TI = '1' and
  Year_SI = 2007 then Amount_NU else 0 end) as [Period 01],
;;;;;;;;;;;;;;;;;;;;;;;;;;;;;;;;;;;;;;;;;;;;;;;;;;;;;;;;;;;;;;;;;;;;;;;;
;;;;;;;;;;;;;;;;;;;;;;;;;;;;;;;;;;;;;;;;;;;;;;;;;;;;;;;;;;;;;;;;;;;;;;;;

  sum(case when FA_Category_VC = 'Cost' and Period_TI = '12' and
  Year_SI = 2007 then Amount_NU else 0 end) as [Period 12],
  sum(case when FA_Category_VC = 'Cost' and Year_SI = 2007
  then Amount_NU else 0 end) as [YTD]

from FixedAsset_T join Journal_T on
FixedAsset_T.Doc_No_VC = Journal_T.Doc_No_VC
where FA_Type_VC ='CE'
and Descrip_VC = 'Purchase CompEquip'
group by FA_Type_VC,FA_ID_IN
```

On our next block of query, we place the static text 'Disposal' on the first column; next we place the asset id on the second column. We then pull and sum up the disposal records from the Journal Table, and place it on the appropriate columns, specifying the category name as 'DispCost', and period as '1' in the year equals to 2007. We also need to specify the asset type and description, after joining the FixedAsset Table with the Journals Table, as we only want to extract the records that are related to computer equipment.

```
union all

select FA_Type_VC + ' Disposal' as [Description],FA_ID_IN,
  sum(case when FA_Category_VC = 'DispCost' and Period_TI = '1' and
```

```
  Year_SI = 2007 then Amount_NU else 0 end) as [Period 01],
;;;;;;;;;;;;;;;;;;;;;;;;;;;;;;;;;;;;;;;;;;;;;;;;;;;;;;;;;;;;;;;;;;;;;
;;;;;;;;;;;;;;;;;;;;;;;;;;;;;;;;;;;;;;;;;;;;;;;;;;;;;;;;;;;;;;;;;;;;;

  sum(case when FA_Category_VC = 'DispCost' and Period_TI = '12' and
  Year_SI = 2007 then Amount_NU else 0 end) as [Period 12],
  sum(case when FA_Category_VC = 'DispCost' and Year_SI = 2007
  then Amount_NU else 0 end) as [YTD]

from FixedAsset_T join Journal_T on
FixedAsset_T.Doc_No_VC = Journal_T.Doc_No_VC
where FA_Type_VC ='CE'
and Descrip_VC = 'CE DispCost'
group by FA_Type_VC,FA_ID_IN
```

Our last block of query would, add up the amount from our first block and second block, in arriving at a net amount. So, in our query, we would specify the asset category to include both Cost and DispCost, in order to pull the records for purchasing and disposing the computer equipment from the Journal Table.

```
union all

select FA_Type_VC + ' Net Cost' as [Description],FA_ID_IN,
 sum(case when FA_Category_VC in ('Cost','DispCost') and
 Period_TI = '1' and Year_SI = 2007
 then Amount_NU else 0 end) as [Period 01],
;;;;;;;;;;;;;;;;;;;;;;;;;;;;;;;;;;;;;;;;;;;;;;;;;;;;;;;;;;;;;;;;;;;;;
;;;;;;;;;;;;;;;;;;;;;;;;;;;;;;;;;;;;;;;;;;;;;;;;;;;;;;;;;;;;;;;;;;;;;

  sum(case when FA_Category_VC in ('Cost','DispCost') and
  Period_TI = '12' and Year_SI = 2007
  then Amount_NU else 0 end) as [Period 12],
  sum(case when FA_Category_VC in ('Cost','DispCost') and
  Year_SI = 2007 then Amount_NU else 0 end) as [YTD]

from FixedAsset_T join Journal_T on
FixedAsset_T.Doc_No_VC = Journal_T.Doc_No_VC
where FA_Type_VC ='CE'
and Descrip_VC in ('Purchase CompEquip','CE DispCost')
group by FA_Type_VC,FA_ID_IN
```

Summary

In Chapter 13, we have learned how to create reports from the Asset Table, applying the Transact-SQL to perform the select query to produce the necessary accounting reports required by MaxCorp.

To summarize, in this chapter, we have discussed:

> How to create select query to produce an Asset Summary

> How to create select query to produce an Asset Movement Report

Conclusion

We have completed the task of designing and creating tables from Chapter 1 to Chapter 7, for a functional accounting database. By now, you would have learnt the steps of normalization to refining individual data structure into an integrated model that suits MaxCorp's business process and reporting requirement.

In confirming the functionality and usability of our database, we conducted a few SQL report for each accounting modules we have developed for MaxCorp. We have learnt the techniques of writing sql scripts for each of the reports requested by Dave.

In reality, there are many other factors that requires significant consideration in defining and designing accounting database, for example, front-end integration, third-party application interface, data warehousing and other business process elements that are unique to each different types of industries.

The above information given is an indispensable facts and the tools and procedures contained in each of the above chapters will provide value-added knowledge to software engineer, database developer, accountant and even to university students who are interested in accounting database design.

Free Accounting Software : If you are interested in using a free bookkeeping software, you may try downloading a copy of DES from the author's official website at http://www.accountingdes.com.

15737387R00090

Made in the USA
Lexington, KY
13 June 2012